Capital Controls in Emerging Economies

The Political Economy of Global Interdependence
Thomas D. Willett, Series Editor

Capital Controls in Emerging Economies, edited by Christine P. Ries and Richard J. Sweeney

Judging Economic Policy: Selected Writings of Gottfried Haberler, edited by Richard J. Sweeney, Edward Tower, and Thomas D. Willett

Political Capacity and Economic Behavior, edited by Marina Arbetman and Jacek Kugler

Interest Groups and Monetary Integration: The Political Economy of Exchange Regime Choice, Carsten Hefeker

Growth, Debt, and Politics: Economic Adjustment and the Political Performance of Developing Countries, Lewis W. Snider

Establishing Monetary Stability in Emerging Market Economies, edited by Thomas D. Willett, Richard C.K. Burdekin, Richard J. Sweeney, and Clas Wihlborg

Closure in International Politics: The Impact of Strategy, Blocs, and Empire, John A. Kroll

Toward a North American Community? Canada, the United States, and Mexico, edited by Donald Barry, with Mark O. Dickerson and James D. Gaisford

Seeking Common Ground: Canada-U.S. Trade Dispute Settlement Policies in the Nineties, Andrew D.M. Anderson

The Political Economy of European Monetary Unification, edited by Barry Eichengreen and Jeffry Frieden

Capital Controls in Emerging Economies

EDITED BY

Christine P. Ries and Richard J. Sweeney

WestviewPress
A Division of HarperCollins*Publishers*

The Political Economy of Global Interdependence

Published in 1997 in the United States of America by Westview Press, 5500 Central Avenue, Boulder, Colorado 80301-2877, and in the United Kingdom by Westview Press, 12 Hid's Copse Road, Cumnor Hill, Oxford OX2 9JJ

Library of Congress Cataloging-in-Publication Data
Capital controls in emerging economies / edited by Christine P. Ries
and Richard J. Sweeney.
p. c.m.— (The political economy of global interdependence :
174)
Includes bibliographical references (p.).
ISBN 0-8133-8907-0
1. Capital movements. 2. Monetary policy. 3. Capital market.
4. Corporations—Finance. I. Hekman, Christine Ries, 1947– .
II. Sweeney, Richard J. (Richard James, 1944– . III. Series.
HG3891.C357 1997
332'.041—dc21 97-18280
CIP

The paper used in this publication meets the requirements of the American National Standard for Permanence of Paper for Printed Library Materials Z39.48-1984.

10 9 8 7 6 5 4 3 2 1

This book is dedicated to my mother, Etta Lillian Bergmann Ries, with deepest gratitude for her love and support.

This book is dedicated to my parents, John and Catherine Sweeney, with love.

Contents

Preface

As this book comes to print, we find that the issues discussed here and the combination of approaches used are more generally applicable than we had imagined. When we began the project from which this book derives, we were very intrigued with events taking place in Central and Eastern Europe and the Soviet Union. We realized that the challenges confronted and the dynamics to be played out by the peoples of this region were outside the realms both of our experience and of the historical record. As a result, we were forced to adopt an improvisational approach to the design of our research. As we realized additional complexities in the situation that we studied and the situation itself evolved, we reached out to involve representatives of other disciplines in our work.

As this summary of our work is drawn, we realize that the approaches we developed in this study are applicable to a broad range of seemingly unrelated economic, social and political problems. These approaches stimulate new approaches and new partnerships as we consider problems of policy in emerging markets for new technologies in developed and developing countries alike.

The underlying questions addressed in this book are two. First, what are the effects of government intervention in a private market when the institutions that support that market are in the early stages of development? Second, how might such intervention be used in concert with other policies to promote the objective of economic development?

Debates about the consequences of government intervention in private markets have been longstanding. Since the questions are so broad and the unintended consequences so pervasive, professionals and scholars have not been able to come to a single conclusion. Rather, we examine possibilities for government intervention situation by situation. The best we can do is to look for common elements in these situations and hope to derive answers for various categories of problems.

In this volume, we look at situations where a dramatic transformation of the political environment made existing institutions obsolete. Social and economic instability made the development of new institutions and networks in business and government essential. We found in these cases that government intervention was potentially much stronger and more pervasive than in situations we have traditionally studied. Further, such intervention was likely to have more permanent effects because it alters the structures of institutions as they form rather than after they are fully established.

As it happens, the elements of complexity and transformation that characterize the "emerging markets" of the formerly communist countries are present in the policy problems of more countries and in more situations than we had imagined. Given the extent of technological and social change that has stimulated demands for new policy around the world, this should not have surprised us. However, as we preface this volume, the single message we convey is that the approaches described in these chapters have relevance for challenges that reach far afield of the countries that informed our work.

For instance, the insights derived from the essays in this book have caused us to view problems of economic development in areas of both rural and urban poverty in the United States from completely new perspectives. When confronted with questions regarding appropriate legal and regulatory changes in the area of banking and financial services, we now rely on many of the useful constructs and connections that are described in these pages. This work has also caused us to be more critical and less accepting of traditional answers to long-standing policy dilemmas. As we were forced to confront questions of policy in situations where complexity and volatility were the bywords, we were forced into collaboration at the deepest levels of our disciplines. Our work has been truly interdisciplinary as well as multidisciplinary. We find ourselves more aware of the interdisciplinary aspects of almost all the problems we have faced since the completion of this research on emerging markets.

This work has also made the disciplines espoused by our collaborators more accessible to us. Thus, we find ourselves better able to work in cross-disciplinary teams and less sanguine about research and policy that are founded on the paradigm of a single discipline.

In summary, we have found that the insights and approaches that we and our colleagues developed through the work described in this book has informed our work in many other areas of study. We hope that as you read these chapters you will experience at least some of the perturbation of complacency that has made new areas of study come alive for us.

Christine P. Ries and Richard J. Sweeney

Acknowledgments

The articles in this volume were solicited from participants in a series of conferences organized to explore the emergence and integration into the global community of countries from Central and Eastern Europe and the former Soviet Union. The core group of scholars that participated in these conferences and in the research and travel that supported our discussions felt especially privileged to have engaged in these studies at the early stages of liberalization. As our project began early and extended over several years, we were able to observe first hand extraordinary developments that have challenged our fundamental assumptions about market economics and greatly enriched our approaches to the study of markets and institutions.

This volume, completed two years after our last conference, contains a summary of those insights. Taken together, the articles contained here challenge us to reach beyond the edges of our disciplinary boundaries. This challenge implies that academic research which is intended to yield relevant and influential results will increasingly be produced by scholars working in teams. Without the inclusion of a range of backgrounds and perspectives, scholarship suffers from a potentially dangerous myopia. Nowhere is this more true than in social and economic situations where institutions are emerging or restructuring and individuals' behaviors are complex. We were fortunate to have a team that represented not only a range of backgrounds and interests, but also a set of enjoyable and open-minded colleagues. Two individuals have our gratitude and admiration for developing that team and for organizing the conferences and research travel.

Professor Thomas D. Willett, Horton Professor of Economics at Claremont Graduate University and Claremont McKenna College, was the "soul" of the project. His energetic and creative recruitment of scholars from many institutions and backgrounds attests to his good judgement and vision. Tom brought us together and plunged us into an exciting arena of social and intellectual change. He organized the travel and conferences in a way that promoted collaboration and intense discussion across a wide range of topics. He hounded us to develop the insights that connected the discussions and to finish the papers. He guided and pleaded as we began to understand the implications of our work for numerous areas of public and corporate policy and to organize the papers into volumes that would make these insights available to others.

Professor Clas Wihlborg, Felix Neuberg Professor at Göteborg University, served much the same function from his bases in Sweden and the United States and recruited to our group many wonderful scholars from the countries of the former Soviet Union. Through his efforts, we have developed friendships and academic relationships that have enriched us all and hold the promise of much future collaboration. Clas's facility at building relationships was well known to us all even before we began work on this project. However, his ability to arrange logistics in times and places where western convention and travel facilities had yet to penetrate amazed us all.

Professor Vello Vensel and his colleagues at Tallinn Technical University also deserve special credit for their wonderful hospitality and support. Vello opened doors to us and, together with his wonderful wife, Lia, helped us to appreciate more fully the history and courage of the people of these emerging countries. Through them, and the people they introduced us to, we have come to hold these peoples, especially the people of Estonia, in our hearts and minds.

We are particularly grateful to Vello and to his students and the alumni of Tallinn Technical University for inviting us to present a workshop on decision making in market economies. The Estonian bankers, business people and policymakers who participated in this exciting three-day event helped us fully appreciate how different were the set of constraints that these people face as they push their institutions toward greater democracy and prosperity.

Many other colleagues participated in our discussions and played no small part in the development of the scholarship presented in this volume. In addition to the authors, special thanks go to Professor Kimball Dietrich and Professor Frank Wycoff.

Ms. Pamela Martin provided patient and untiring support in the editing and typesetting of the volume. Her background as a Ph.D. student in Claremont's Economics Program prepared her for the careful and thoughtful contributions that she made to clarify our prose and make our thoughts more accessible.

Finally, none of our work would have been possible without the generous financial support of the Lincoln Foundation, funds from the Georgetown Seminar Series in Finance at Georgetown University and Göteborg University.

Christine P. Ries and Richard J. Sweeney

Capital Controls in Emerging Economies

Introduction and Overview

Christine P. Ries

Until recently, capital controls were considered by many policymakers to be among the more arcane and technical instruments of economic policy. National governments frequently imposed controls in support of balance of payments and monetary policy objectives when international capital flows threatened to overwhelm domestic policy priorities. The appropriateness of their application in these conditions, or the extension of their use to other situations, was little discussed. In the last decade, however, the power of market-based economics has swept through formerly socialist and communist countries, leading to economic and political reform in many of these states. With these changes, debates over the use of capital controls have gained new prominence since capital controls have frequently been used to sequence and fine tune liberalization policies in the emerging market economies.

The essays in this book should convince the reader that debates about the role and impact of capital controls can no longer be relegated to the offices of "policy wonks" and economists who specialize in international monetary policy. Rather, as political and economic institutions are transformed within a global setting, decisions to divert or distort the flow of global capital have pervasive and long lasting impacts on the basic structures of national economies. Capital controls are not tangential but fundamental elements of economic policy and management.

Capital controls, far from being an arcane tool for fine tuning economic policy and macroeconomic or balance of payments management, are shown to be of central relevance in determining patterns of international ownership and the character of national private investment. They can also have a significant effect on patterns of population migration and the development of national comparative advantage. They affect industrial organization at the deepest levels and so should be of concern to corporate strategists, investment portfolio managers and equity traders, and anyone concerned with such broad issues of public policy as development and growth, education, and infrastructure planning.

In the following chapters several noted economists present their thoughts about the use of capital controls in the reforming economies of the formerly communist countries. In addition, the collection of analytical approaches presented here offers important insights about the formation of basic institutions and the essentials of public policy analysis in dynamic political and economic settings.

One important lesson learned from the study of capital controls in emerging market economies is that controls can have pervasive, lasting impact on an economy and society if the restrictions are in place while basic institutions and infrastructure are developing. While much of the literature on this subject deals with the speed and sequencing of liberalization, this book extends our understanding of the permanent impact of even temporary controls.

We also learn several important lessons about the study of public policy in situations where not only economic, but also political and social institutions are in a state of flux. In the dynamic and complex environments of emerging markets, our work must demonstrate the effects of any policy choices on the individual decisions that determine patterns of investment, ownership, employment and economic development. In order to understand and predict these relationships we must explicitly describe the transmission of macroeconomic variations into the microeconomics of decision making. This allows us to describe the relationship between financial variables and real economic, social, and political outcomes. Finally, in order to address this range of issues and interactions, we must draw upon several traditionally distinct literatures and develop analytical approaches that incorporate the most useful features of each.

General Lessons for Policy Analysis in Dynamic and Restructuring Economies

Perhaps the greatest change in the global economic system since 1945 has been the explosive growth in capital flows and capital mobility between nations. Our traditional approaches to questions of capital control evolved from a time when trade flows dominated the public attention and public policy was focused on the relative status and well being of producers and consumers at home and abroad.

Today, it is much more widely understood that global capital flows can drive both instability and economic growth. Investment funding is generally seen as the basis for the development of infrastructure and national productive capacity. It is also clear that access to global financial markets is a necessity given the magnitude of investment required for economic development. Finally, international investment flows and trade in ownership claims carry with them information, transfers of technology, intellectual capital, and managerial talent.

As capital flows have come to dominate international trade flows, and to carry with them so many intangibles such as issues of ownership and transfers of technology, so must our intellectual orientation expand as we propose and assess public policy. From the literature written for corporate financial managers and the financial services industries we learn that the forces of global arbitrage and the emergence of new financial markets and services exert a strong influence on the allocation of investment funds. This work allows us to understand the channels by which arbitrage is conducted and to elucidate the linkages between economic development projects and individual investors. We can understand and predict how global investors will assess those differences in risk and return that are inherent in a particular national social and economic setting.

The reality of global arbitrage also confronts us with a powerful fact: Nations and governments that pursue economic development and prosperity are in direct competition with other nations and even large corporations for the funding that supports such growth.

From this perspective we are better able to model and measure the transmission of changes in aggregate variables such as interest rates or foreign exchange rates into the individual investment and operating decisions that ultimately determine aggregate growth and prosperity. That is, taking the perspective of global financial arbitrage and financial market structures, we are able to assess the linkages between micro- and macroeconomics and between the real and financial sectors. Our work in emerging markets and the essays presented in this book demonstrate that an understanding of these linkages is central to the formation of effective economic policy.

The literature on capital markets and corporate finance has also yielded a perspective on economic and organizational restructuring and revitalization that is highly relevant to emerging market activity. Cross-border investment flows carry not only funding for development projects, but also components of ownership and control. Issues of ownership and control pull us beyond the issues of nationalism and mercantilism to concerns about decision making, incentives, and productivity.

The exploration of these economic insights together with unavoidable political challenges suggests new formats and new perspectives for policy analysis. In this book we present analytical models and analysis that account for the public and private, the real and financial sectors, nationalism and productivity against a background of democratic political systems.

Finally, taken together the approaches presented in the chapters that follow enable us to better predict the effects of particular economic policies in complex and multifaceted settings and where individual agents or decision makers adapt their behavior in response to policy. By focusing on the particular setting of emerging economies, we were forced to account for the adaptability that comes as decision makers gain freedom of choice and access to information.

In addition, because the countries we studied were small and their political systems nascent, all of the interactions and decisions are more complex than for large, well-established countries. Clearly, the approaches developed here for addressing capital controls in rapidly changing and complex environments have many lessons for sophisticated policy analysis of other dynamic and complex settings.

Implications for Parliamentary Structure and Control of Public Policy

The lessons of this book may also be extended to consider the process by which public policy is formed, assessed and adopted. One implication of our work is that the imposition of capital controls, and perhaps the parliamentary and institutional procedures by which they are imposed, should be discussed with the broadest possible range of representatives from the impacted sectors and other interested parties.[1] Not only the direct but the indirect and long-term consequences must be fully and explicitly explored. The details of our analysis can also be used to develop a list of individuals and groups that may be convened as political constituencies in support of various policies.

The analysis also raises important concerns for environments that are changing rapidly. In such markets, basic institutions are still unformed or malleable and changing patterns of social and political affiliation create a dynamic environment. Patterns of trade, channels of marketing and distribution, and the ownership and control of productive assets evolve rapidly.

In such settings, public policies are potentially more powerful than where existing institutional arrangements constrain decision makers on all sides. When policy decisions can influence the very foundations of institutional arrangements, they can be expected to have a much more enduring impact than is usually the case, for good or ill. The natural balances and corrective mechanisms inherent in well-developed institutional arrangements may not be present in emerging market countries.

These natural balances existing in the more mature democracies—and absent in the emerging market economies—mitigate the effects of changes in both political and economic spheres. In the emerging market economies, long-established interest groups or constituencies with an interest in preserving past privileges may dominate policy discussions, and groups with a greater stake in the future may not be adequately represented. In addition, the former may use their position to cement themselves in power as new institutions are formed.

On the economic side, shallow markets for credit and other risk management instruments mean that any given change in a macroeconomic variable will have a more substantial effect on the real sector of the economy. For example, changes in interest rates will have a greater impact on the availability of credit to small and growing enterprises in economies where a broader range of security offerings is not open to the borrower.

These aspects of the emerging market situation present special challenges to analysts of economic policy. We are dealing with settings that are dynamic and fluid. The transmission of changes in macroeconomic variables has greater and longer lasting effects on microeconomic or individual behavior. Decision makers are more heavily influenced by a few basic aggregate variables than is the case where fully developed markets and institutions offer a range of alternative solutions for investment and operating problems.

Liberalizing Markets: An Overview

Liberalizing countries face the issue of "sequencing" as they determine the order of markets to be opened to international competition. At one extreme is the "big bang" approach where product and financial markets are liberalized domestically and at the same time opened to foreign competition. In practice, many successful liberalization experiences have eschewed this approach for a more gradual process of liberalization. Most often, market pricing, profits, and private ownership are first accepted in internal markets with allowance for imports and international competition to follow. At some point, financial markets are opened domestically and internationally, but national banking and financial services are usually protected well into the liberalization process. In addition, restrictions on the inflow and outflow of capital owned by foreigners are usually lifted before the elimination of restrictions on domestic residents' ability to invest capital abroad.

In "Orthodoxy Is Right: Liberalize the Capital Account Last," John Williamson supports the sequence of liberalization outlined above. A key reason for delay in liberalizing foreign capital flows is the possibility that massive inflows and outflows might destabilize financial markets and thus disrupt product markets before reforms are fully established and firms have become strong enough to endure financial shocks. In particular, large capital outflows may drive domestic interest rates so high that credit is largely unobtainable for most firms, and these firms, which are likely to have weak balance sheets in the early stages of liberalization, are unlikely to survive. Or, massive capital inflows may lead to such strong exchange rate appreciation that domestic firms cannot sell profitably in international markets or compete against imports. Reducing the possibilities of such disruptions justifies delay in capital account liberalization until producers are strong enough to face capital account shocks. Of course, restrictions on foreign capital flows are likely to reduce overall investment in the liberalizing country, and thus restrictions should be progressively relaxed as product-market liberalization becomes more strongly entrenched. Similarly, restrictions on domestic residents' outflows to reduce the possibilities of destabilizing capital flows can be relaxed as product-market liberalization is strengthened.

In "Reality and the Logic of Capital Flow Liberalization," Manuel Guitián argues that this sequencing strategy is misconceived. While interventions that restrict the international flow of capital are currently accepted as tools of international policy, Guitián argues that the acceptability of capital controls is an artifact of the past. As we approach the twenty-first century, capital controls are far more likely to disrupt than to facilitate effective and efficient global economic integration and expansion. In today's environment, trade flows are relatively well established and capital flows are increasingly important to the effective functioning of the global economy.

A simplifying and powerful perspective is presented in Guitián's argument for parallel treatment of current account or trade transactions and capital transactions. He reviews the strong and generally accepted reasons for promotion of current account convertibility or free trade in goods. These same arguments should also be applied, he argues, to trade in capital—trade in financial securities. In parallel with free trade, freedom of capital movements will enhance economic efficiency, promote growth, and increase wealth.

Another persuasive argument for the removal of restrictions on capital flows is related to the underlying health of the domestic economy. Capital controls are imposed in order to insulate the domestic economy from external economic shocks or in order to preserve domestic economic distortions, including "prevailing sources of imbalance and of inappropriate policies." Capital controls mask the effects of these distortions and can actually cause the distortions to become institutionalized. The distortions prevail, often with widespread, negative, and unintended effect.

One implication of Guitián's argument is that public policy analysis in this arena should be shifted from a preoccupation with the effects of exchange rate changes on the balance of trade to focus on the effects of capital flows on domestic investment growth and performance. This approach would also argue for attention to policies that promote flexibility and responsiveness rather than those that reward inflexibility.

Finally, as a byproduct of the argument for capital mobility, we are offered an informed view of economic history that not only explains the international acceptance of capital controls, but offers interesting insights into the makings of international monetary institutions and international agreements.

"Preconditions for Liberalization of Capital Flows—A Review and Interpretation," by Clas Wihlborg and Kalman Deszeri provides a review of the scholarly background to which the other chapters implicitly speak. Their survey describes wide-spread agreement that both developing and industrialized countries should support full capital mobility, though limits to convertibility and sequencing may still depend on some preconditions in the economy for effective implementation. Much of the more current literature discusses these preconditions and the underlying causes of conditions that would prevent full convertibility. Wihlborg and Deszeri suggest that the limits to full liberalization may come from either market failures or policy limitations or both, and their comprehensive review of the literature shows how each argument depends on a basic assumption about market and policy failures. They argue that some criteria for liberalization, such as sufficient revitalization of privatized industries, may delay capital account liberalization for an excessive and perhaps indefinite period. Like Guitián, they relate the discussion to an analysis of failures in commercial or trade policy that shows why authorities may apply a "second best" policy because of implementation limitations.

Finally, their chapter leads us into the broader perspective that is addressed in succeeding chapters. In recognizing the financial underpinnings for capital flows, they suggest that analysis that fails to account for investor expectations and risk will lead to biased and erroneous prescriptions.

"The Information Costs of Capital Controls" by Richard Sweeney introduces the second section of this book. While the chapters in the first section provided background and framework, those in the second section introduce and develop new perspectives. Sweeney's paper leads off by assessing one of the other roles of the financial system: to provide information for a broad range of business and investment decisions. Sweeney concludes that this role is sufficiently important to push the sequencing argument strongly in favor of early liberalization for capital transactions.

By pricing financial securities, the capital markets perform many functions in the economy. One of the most important is to provide information about the size and costs of various risks. When functioning capital markets are fully open, managers and investors can use the information contained in the patterns of security prices to assess the risks inherent in particular assets. Without this information, each assessment and each decision conceivably requires very extensive data collection, analysis and calculation. Since, in reality, these calculations cannot be effectively made, the quality of the resulting decisions is greatly compromised.

When, however, local and national economies are fully integrated into the global economy, capital markets are free to assess information and security pricing is fair, the information assessment burden is manageable. Rather than starting from scratch, each decision maker can simply observe market prices and make incremental adjustments for differences in the project under consideration. This chapter presents the conceptual and mathematical arguments and shows the magnitude of the estimation costs that must be borne by decisions makers in countries where markets are isolated from global pricing.

Within the scheme of this book this chapter makes an important transition. An essential assumption for the mathematical development is that international financial arbitrage is a force to be reckoned with. Sweeney shows us how our policy analysis must be reoriented when arbitrage forces are dominant, as they have certainly become in recent decades.

Working further into the analysis of information and risk, Sweeney considers the importance of government credibility in this process. He shows that lack of credibility undermines the entire pricing process and significantly reduces the value to be gained by more immediate liberalization. He demonstrates that credibility is damaged when controls are retained for domestic investors even though investment transactions for foreigners are freed. With this discussion, the chapter introduces issues of credibility that are later addressed and extended in the chapters by Dickinson and Mullineux and Wihlborg and Willett.

In "Currency Convertibility, Policy Credibility, and Capital Flight in Poland and Czech and Slovak Federal Republic" David Dickinson and Andrew Mullineux connect the discussion of capital controls to a broad range of other macroeconomic policies. They discuss various types of convertibility and show how these represent attempts to manage both exchange rates and capital flows. By addressing the specific arrangements by which convertibility is controlled and the range of possible responses, their essay places the issue of capital controls firmly at the center of a complex global economic and political system.

Their discussion of the specific ways that convertibility policies interact with this complex, global system shows that today's economic agents have almost unlimited opportunity to pursue global arbitrage opportunities. That is, "effective" capital outflow may occur even if convertibility is lifted and controls are tight. For example, capital controls often stimulate the "dollarization" of the economy. Though not traditionally thought of as capital outflow, "dollarization" has identical effects. The strength and magnitude of this effective outflow is directly related to the appropriateness of the level of the exchange rate.

Dickinson and Mullineux broaden the discussion further as they recognize that capital may flow in *both* directions as economic adjustment and liberalization proceed and that each direction may be problematic. In acknowledging that overshooting may occur, these authors provide the macroeconomic perspective underlying the issues of risk as addressed in the previous chapter by Richard Sweeney. The essay also anticipates the discussion of the effects of risk on capital investment decisions that is presented in Christine Ries's following essay.

Dickinson and Mullineux augment our consideration of the conceptual issues relating to sequencing and capital flows by examining evidence on capital flight in the early stages of economic liberalization in Poland, the Czech Republic and Slovakia. They develop measures of capital flight and trace these in relationship to macroeconomic problems and government credibility in these cases. Their conclusion is that investor uncertainty over political possibilities causes capital flows that exceed what might be expected due to normal investor reshuffling of portfolios.

With this last analysis and discussion, Dickinson and Mullineux's essay moves us to the next stage. Their work anticipates a new policy perspective regarding the control of capital flows. When international arbitrage forces are strong, governments may best be advised to abandon defensive postures in favor of positive and accommodating positions. Even if capital can be effectively restrained, the costs are large. As Sweeney shows, the detrimental and pervasive effect on information flows and analysis alone are sufficient to argue for more immediate capital account liberalization. Dickinson and Mullineux's work strongly suggests that governments are better advised to recognize that global capital resources will flow toward attractive investment opportunities. Rather than attempt to constrain capital flows, governments might more effectively achieve investment and growth targets by attending to their attractiveness as hosts for investment and operations.

In "Capital Controls and Corporate Investment Behavior" Christine Ries pushes this argument more fully to the level of specific decision making and examines the microeconomic implications. Using the theory of corporate finance, she assesses the effects of tight capital controls on the structure of ownership and industrial development. When such controls have the effect of raising the returns required by investors, they reduce the total amount of capital investment in the country. Further, if domestic investors are especially penalized by being denied opportunities to diversify their risks through investment in foreign markets, the risk that they effectively bear for any given project is higher than the risk borne by foreign investors.

When this bias against domestic investors is sufficiently large, foreigners gain the advantage in bidding for projects that have lower risk and greater long-term growth prospects. They accept higher up-front costs and are initially willing to commit larger amounts of capital and to postpone their gains over a longer period.

These patterns of investment have important implications for the future corporate and asset ownership patterns within the country. Foreigners are likely to be charged with "buying up" the country both because of their large initial investments and because the value of the investments will grow more over time. Depending on the degree of bias, one will see domestic ownership concentrated in industries that quickly become "mature" while foreign ownership will dominate in industries that constitute the growth sector. The same bias affects all operating and internal investment decisions and places domestic owners and investors at an increasing disadvantage in terms of employee training and recruitment, investment in new technology, and expansion of employment opportunities. The analysis can be extended even to address issues of population migration with implications for the types of employment opportunities and immigration the capital control policies will encourage.

The chapter demonstrates the many ways that capital controls change investment and operating decisions and shows that a country that adopts these investment and operating decisions and shows that a country that adopts these controls may be buying significant social and political problems in the future.

"Capital Account Liberalization and Policy Incentives: An Endogenous Policy View" contributes insights from the fields of public choice and rational choice economics. This perspective emphasizes the endogenous roles of policymakers: policies influence markets and markets influence policies. Clas Wihlborg and Thomas Willett emphasize that a complete analysis requires recognition of this endogenous component. One implication is that policies may be more credible if the institutional context imposes high costs on government actions that violate trust or exceed the bounds of good judgment. For example, domestic monetary authorities may be effectively constrained by fear of negative market reactions to monetary growth rates that are perceived as excessive.

Similarly, conclusions about the impetus for and effects of speculative crises depend on whether capital flows are seen as the triggers for crisis or whether the flow of capital is seen as a symptomatic response to more basic policy initiatives. Does an exogenous reorientation of investment flows cause an economic crisis, or does the cause reside in some deeper flaw in basic public policy? The policy prescription in times of crisis or as prophylactic policy must depend on the answer to this question.

If significant capital outflow represents flight from poor policies, the prescription is to change the underlying policy. However, if capital outflow is exogenous and unwarranted, it may be appropriate to institute capital controls or other policies to slow or stop that outflow.

Michael Dooley's chapter, "A Payments Mechanism for the Independent States of the Former Soviet Union," addresses a fundamental aspect of international capital flows—the payments mechanism for international transactions. This case study, however, focuses directly on the agents most strongly affected by the economic and social transformation. It considers the development of payments mechanisms *between* states that are newly independent but were formerly part of the USSR. In essence, this is trade that was formerly interstate, but is now international.

Dooley raises considerations of both economics and politics. His objective is to design a payments mechanism that shifts trade patterns as little as possible from the most efficient outcome. "The basic idea is that...the payments mechanism should get in the way as little as possible." Dooley provides details regarding the direction of trade between republics and discusses the mechanics required to finance this trade. He then considers the various political arrangements required to bring about the appropriate policies and institutions.

As a final chapter, this essay takes us into the specifics of one area where capital liberalization directly affects trading transactions and economic well being. Dooley draws explicitly the connection between the financial market structure and the facility of trade in goods. He shows the roles that national governments must play in effecting orderly and efficient transitions. Finally, this piece demonstrates again the range of issues and considerations that must come into play as policy analysts debate controls on the flows of capital and other capital market interventions in an era of dynamic transformation and complex change.

Notes

1. Here we implicitly assume that those in control of public policy seek policies to benefit the whole country, rather than to benefit select individuals and groups at the expense of the whole. Further, this discussion assumes that the range of representatives to a discussion are sufficiently focused to support the development of a consensus.

1

Orthodoxy Is Right: Liberalize the Capital Account Last

John Williamson

Analysis has not so far yielded many robust propositions about the desirable sequencing of liberalizing economic reforms. At one time it was conventional wisdom that stabilization should precede liberalization, based on the evidence of the Bhagwati-Krueger multicountry study that trade liberalization failed if attempted under conditions of macroeconomic disarray. Then Bolivia and Poland demonstrated the important synergies between simultaneous stabilization and liberalization, and a "big bang" became a respectable option. Other robust recommendations have been hard to come by, and policy advice has tended to be reduced to doing everything just as soon as feasible.

There remains one exception. It has long been argued that the capital account of the balance of payments should be one of the last things to be liberalized. There are good reasons for this recommendation, and they remain valid.

Inflows: The Sequencing Literature

The literature does not challenge the proposition that the first-best situation involves an open capital account. What it does do is to identify four dangers of liberalizing the capital account before other parts of the economy have been liberalized. It is thus a standard application of the theory of the second best.

The first danger is that liberalizing capital inflows before trade has been liberalized will cause capital to flow into the wrong, i.e., import-substituting, industries. A classic article of Brecher and Diaz Alejandro (1977) showed that such a capital inflow must be immiserizing.

A second danger is that the liberalization of capital inflows before the domestic financial system has been liberalized will lead to an inefficient allocation of investment.

A third danger is that liberalization of capital inflows before the establishment of fiscal discipline will serve only to provide temporary financing for budget deficits that are ultimately unsustainable, and whose correction will be more costly and painful the longer it is delayed. Borrowing simply serves to magnify the size of the future crisis.

The final danger is that capital inflows will serve to appreciate the real value of the currency and thus end the export-led growth that provides the only viable way for countries to develop. This danger does not fall quite as naturally into the standard second-best mold as the others, since it is caused by market myopia rather than by government-imposed distortions and may remain a problem even after an economy has been thoroughly liberalized. That is one of the reasons some of us favor exchange-rate management for industrial as well as developing countries. In my judgment it is worth accepting the intensification of the difficulty of exchange-rate management caused by a liberal capital account once nontraditional export industries are securely established, but not until then.

The failure of the liberalization programs implemented in the Southern Cone in the late 1970s demonstrated that these dangers are far from hypothetical (indeed, it was that failure that motivated the development of the analysis). The high cost of New Zealand's liberalization program, which again started with a liberalization of the capital account, has provided a subsequent confirmation of the analysis.

Outflows

Note that all four of the concerns identified in the sequencing literature relate to the dangers of excessive capital *inflows*. This is not, however, the current concern in Eastern Europe. Let us therefore turn to consider the less-explored but more relevant problem of outflows.

The main reason that countries seek to control capital outflows is to avoid a loss of savings that could be invested in the domestic economy. The answer to the obvious question as to why it should be socially advantageous to invest at home even though asset holders find it privately preferable to invest abroad is that there are risks to domestic investment that can be overcome only through collective action that generates a sufficiently high rate of growth to avoid political rejection of the economic order. In Western

Europe in the postwar years we took it for granted that such considerations justified collective action to limit the freedom of wealth owners, and the U.S. government accepted the legitimacy of those actions. The success of postwar recovery suggests that Western Europe was right. We have no right to impose a different set of priorities on Eastern Europe today without compelling reasons for believing either that the region does not need more investment or that capital controls will not help to keep savings at home.

Since the first of those possibilities is a priori preposterous, I presume that the advocates of immediate capital account liberalization believe the second to be true. No one can seriously maintain that capital controls will not leak, but it is not true that they are thereby bound to be totally ineffective. In particular, it is possible to keep institutional savings at home; while institutional savings may be modest at the moment, one should expect them to grow rapidly if the transition begins to succeed.

I agree that at times the relaxation of capital outflow controls has had the paradoxical effect of stimulating a net capital inflow. The reason is that the elimination of outflow controls assures investors that it will not be difficult to get their money out again should they so wish, and in that way reduces the option value of holding funds outside the country (Lában and Larraín 1993). But things do not work out that way if there is a large volume of funds wanting to escape from the country, as Chile found out to its cost in 1982. The situation is clearly similar in Eastern Europe today. Rather than allowing Eastern Europe to import the world interest rate as Richard Sweeney argues (Chapter 4), a sudden liberalization of both sides of the capital account would result in capital outflows until the local interest rate had risen to equality with the world interest rate plus a presumptively large risk premium, with a resulting increase in the shadow price of capital.

I have discussed elsewhere (Williamson 1993) a series of other factors that are potentially relevant in deciding whether to liberalize capital outflows.

1. There is a danger that capital flows will be cyclically destabilizing (in the sense that a negative shock to the current account will provoke capital outflows) until a country has credibly established the permanence of its policy regime. Once that is accomplished, it will be able to use an increase in interest rates to attract capital inflows and thus mitigate the shock. In the best of circumstances, it will take time to establish the credibility of the policy regime in Eastern Europe.
2. Small countries in particular can gain important benefits from portfolio diversification by two-way capital flows. But that becomes feasible only when foreign investors are not deterred by political

risks that apply differentially to them; until that condition is met, which it surely is not as yet in Eastern Europe, the effect of liberalization will be a capital outflow rather than a balanced flow.

3. High capital mobility requires either a floating exchange rate or severe constraints (at the least) on monetary policy. It would in my view be unwise for most of the countries to float freely and thus lose the ability to ensure an exchange rate sufficiently competitive to secure export-led growth. The countries need to keep monetary policy as a usable tool for demand management at least until fiscal policy is in a position to take up the strain.
4. Holding foreign assets is a way to evade taxation, at least until tax administration is strong and the country has established a network of tax treaties with the main potential haven countries. Both things will take time.
5. Countries with large stocks of foreign assets have a strong reason to liberalize capital outflows in order to privatize the foreign investment decision. But Eastern Europe is not, and certainly should not be, anything like a net creditor region.
6. An open capital account exposes the financial sector to the disciplines of foreign competition. However, the domestic financial system needs to be strong enough to compete, not loaded down with nonperforming assets from dinosaur state enterprises as it is in Eastern Europe, before the disciplines of foreign competition can be expected to enhance performance rather than precipitate financial collapse.

Notes

This paper is taken from remarks at a conference on "Capital Controls and Financial Liberalization in Transitioning Economies" held at Georgetown University, April 23, 1993.

References

Brecher, Richard A., and Carlos Diaz Alejandro. 1977. "Tariffs, Foreign Capital, and Immiserizing Growth." *Journal of International Economics* 7(4): 317–22.

Lában, Raúl, and Felipe Larraín. 1993. "Can a Liberalization of Capital Outflows Increase Net Capital Inflows?" PUC-Santiago Documento de Trabajo no. 155.

Williamson, John. 1993. "A Cost-Benefit Analysis of Capital Account Liberalization," in Helmut Reisen and Bernhard Fischer, eds., *Financial Opening*. Pp. 25–34. Paris: Organization for Economic Cooperation and Development.

2

Reality and the Logic of Capital Flow Liberalization

Manuel Guitián

Introduction

The international financial code of conduct negotiated at the Bretton Woods Conference towards the end of the Second World War accepts the use of controls and restrictions on international capital flows by its signatories.[1] At the time of the drafting and adoption of the *Articles of Agreement* it was reasonable to include this particular norm among the rules of the game that were to govern international transactions. The flow of trade and capital among countries had been disrupted in the 1930s and during the war; capital movements had not yet become a predominant force in the international transaction network; and the reconstruction of a normally functioning world economy made the encouragement of international trade and exchange paramount. Consequently, attention was focused on the liberalization of trade and other current account flows, and this focus was reflected in the language of the *Articles of Agreement* of the International Monetary Fund.[2] An additional consideration was the alleged ability of capital controls to preserve the independence of domestic policies. Such ability, though, also provided countries with leeway to pursue inconsistent policies (at least for a time); from this standpoint, capital controls may have been an obstacle to the aims of international policy coordination.

Since the Bretton Woods era, however, international capital movements have acquired increasing importance in the world economy. Although numerous other factors also played a part, the growing relevance of capital flows in the international economy since the 1970s owes much to the opening of trade and current accounts that characterized the evolution of the international economy under the Bretton Woods regime.[3] This period, which extended through the early 1970s, witnessed a progressive liberalization of current international transactions in the industrial countries as well as the corresponding integration of their national economies and those of an increasing number of developing countries into the international system. Establishment of *current account convertibility* was largely attained in the industrial world by the late 1950s or early 1960s.[4] With it, international trade and other current account flows became an increasingly important part of the world economic setting, which became more interdependent as a result.

In what might well be termed a revolt against the constraints of economic interdependence, the Bretton Woods exchange rate system collapsed in the early 1970s, when countries decided to move away from a fixed exchange rate system to a regime of flexible exchange rate arrangements. The shift in focus in world financial relations from an *international standpoint* (which is a central feature of a par value or fixed exchange rate setting) to a *national perspective* (which is typical of a flexible exchange rate framework) augured the appearance of a tendency toward the relative closing of national economies, that is, toward an international environment composed of isolated and insulated national components. Paradoxically, this tendency was to an important extent weakened by the increased mobility of international capital flows, which helped to keep the fabric of the international economic system from unraveling. Thus, in reality, developments in the world economy began to make the prescriptions of the code of conduct irrelevant, and capital flows became a predominant aspect of international economic relations, even though the use of capital controls remained acceptable.[5] The capital account continued to grow in importance into the 1980s, a period when the subject of liberalization of capital movements began to attract attention, both in the developing and the industrial worlds.[6]

This paper stresses the logic of such capital account developments and examines the reasons why the code of conduct for international economic policy should be updated to account for global economic developments. The standpoint of the analysis is basically *normative*, that is, it deals with *what ought to be*, rather than *positive*, a vantage point that stresses instead *what is*. The plan of the paper is as follows. It first describes the evolution of international capital flows and the consequent divergence between the reality of the international economy and the code of conduct that is supposed to guide it. Subsequently, the analysis examines capital controls from the perspective of their costs and benefits and assesses their effectiveness. It then examines the interaction of free capital movements with national macroeconomic policies in general, and with monetary and exchange rate management in particular. This examination is followed by a discussion of the systemic implications of the liberalization of international capital flows. Finally, the main points and conclusions of the analysis are summarized in the conclusion.

The Growing Importance of Capital Flows

An essential development in the international economy since the abandonment of the Bretton Woods order has been the growth of gross and net capital flows and the resulting integration of national financial markets, particularly those in the industrial countries. A number of features have accompanied this expansion. Not only has the growth rate of capital flows exceeded that of international trade flows over the same period, but it has led to and reflects the presence of foreign investors in the domestic capital markets of the main industrial countries, a presence that is there to stay, barring major upheavals in the world economy. And a large portion of this expansion of capital flows has been private, rather than official, in nature, with bank lending and security flows the predominant forms. As for the developing countries, heavy borrowing from international banking sources in the late 1970s was followed, as is well known, by a virtual halt in banking and other related flows in the early 1980s. The cessation of bank credit during the period of resolution of the international debt crisis changed the composition of capital movements from private to official and their nature from voluntary to involuntary.[7]

Possibly the most critical development in the recent evolution of capital movements has been the relaxation of capital controls; most of this occurred as part of a broad liberalization and deregulation of domestic financial markets in industrial countries. These events could not but lead to a growing integration of national and international financial markets, which has been made evident both by the scale of capital flows and by developments in yield differentials: capital movements not only have expanded markedly in magnitude but they have also led to arbitrage transactions which have significantly narrowed the margin for national financial rates of return.[8] In effect, financial market integration has outstripped that of goods markets, which is often hampered by recurrent protectionist pressures.

This is a somewhat paradoxical outcome when viewed from the standpoint of the international code of conduct. The bulk of international efforts to create a liberal system has been channeled toward ensuring the free flow of trade in goods and services and freedom of current account transactions. Not only have the IMF's *Articles of Agreement* stressed the importance of current account convertibility, but the *General Agreement on Tariffs and Trade* (GATT) was specifically established to uphold and foster a liberal code of conduct in the field of international trade. In contrast, although continuing efforts have been made by the OECD to establish an internationally accepted code governing capital transaction liberalization, the rules of the game adopted by the membership of the International Monetary Fund did not include capital account convertibility, that is, freedom of capital transactions. And yet, the evolution of the international economy has been such that capital market integration seems to have run well ahead of trade flows integration.

A number of factors account for the relatively rapid and deep integration of international capital markets. They include elements such as the availability of cross-border global investment opportunities which, to be seized, required intermediation of resources across nations. These trends also allowed for cross-border portfolio and risk diversification and have enhanced the efficiency of investment. All these factors reflect the importance of economic fundamentals in the determination of capital flows. But capital movements are also affected by differences in national policies, as well as by the wedges created by economic distortions that vary across countries. Economic policies are pervasive in their effects, and therefore capital flows may reflect them directly—as is the case, for example, with tax policies or official guarantees—or indirectly—as illustrated by inappropriate macroeconomic policies. Distortions (which in the end amount to the existence of different cost structures across countries) in turn influence the direction and scale of capital flows. Capital will tend to flow toward the destination where the costs are lowest, that is, typically toward havens where the distortions are least important. But possibly a more important factor behind developments in capital movements over the last decade has been the growing willingness of economic policymakers to allow market prices a larger role in the process of resource allocation.[9] The upshot of all these factors and recent trends in capital accounts in the world economy has been that the great advances toward integration of national economies through free trade in goods and services fostered by the Bretton Woods agreements have been followed by economic integration spurred by developments on the capital account side, developments running well ahead of the expectations embedded in the existing code of international financial conduct.

There can be no doubt that the central challenge confronting the membership of the International Monetary Fund at the time of its inception was to ensure the integration of war-ridden and restricted economies into an orderly international economic system. To this end, emphasis was placed on the attainment of freedom of *current account* transactions which, as noted above, became the standard for convertibility. This approach reflected the concern with national economic *competitiveness* and with the retention of *national economic policy autonomy* (hence, the acceptability of capital controls). To a large extent, the effectiveness of the approach that was then taken provided the grounds for the emergence of capital flows on an increasingly important scale. These flows have materialized in the presence—and despite the acceptability—of capital controls, a curious instance of events overtaking the rules intended to govern them.

Arguments for and Against Capital Controls

Interference with international capital transactions has taken a variety of forms, broadly involving exchange restrictions and quantitative limitations on the size of capital movements. Exchange restrictions have typically taken the form of dual or multiple exchange rates or of differential tax treatment of international financial transactions. Quantitative restrictions, in turn, have generally constrained the foreign asset-liability positions of banks and other domestic financial institutions, the domestic operations of foreign financial entities, the external portfolios, direct investments or real estate assets of domestic residents, or the direct investments undertaken by foreigners.

Just as varied as the types of capital controls have been the grounds on which they have been justified. These can be classified into four main categories: reduction of balance of payments instability or undue exchange rate volatility; retention of domestic savings and prevention of excessive foreign ownership of domestic factors of production; taxation of domestic capital and financial transactions; and reinforcement of domestic stabilization and reform efforts.

Much though these lines of reasoning may appear defensible in practice, in theory they are far more debatable. Balance of payments crises or unstable exchange rates can hardly be averted on a sustained basis solely by the adoption and maintenance of capital controls. Fundamentally, external imbalances have roots in sources other than capital movements and, therefore, the imposition of capital restrictions cannot be expected to replace appropriate action to remove the source or sources of the imbalance. Thus, at best, capital controls can only act a palliative to give other essential policy measures time to yield their results. Similarly, capital restrictions are unlikely to retain domestic savings in the absence of appropriate incentives to keep them from spontaneously flowing abroad; here again it must be stressed that, in general, capital flight is caused by factors other than freedom of capital movements and it is toward those factors—rather than to the confinement of that freedom—that policy ought to be addressed. Taxation of capital transactions, if excessive, is unlikely to be offset by capital controls. Clearly whenever such taxation exceeds sufficiently its levels abroad, it becomes imperative that some sort of wedge be created in order to prevent shrinkage of the tax base. The introduction of capital controls can be instrumental to this end, but it must also be acknowledged that their continued effectiveness cannot be assured as long as the incentives to circumvent them prevail. And although an argument can be made in favor of temporary capital controls to support domestic stabilization and reform efforts, in gauging the usefulness of such controls for these purposes, it must also be kept in mind their very presence may well impair the credibility of those efforts.

Arguments in support of capital controls have also been made on the basis of the *costs of capital account openness.* Central to these arguments is the belief that capital flows, if left unfettered, increase economic instability because they magnify rather than offset external shocks. But this instability argument depends not only on whether capital flows act to reinforce or to compensate for shocks, it also hinges on whether the shock is internal or external, permanent or transitory. Once these other nuances are considered, we are again faced with the conclusion that capital controls cannot replace action aimed directly at removing the underlying causes of the instability. Another perceived cost of an open capital account is the limitation it can impose on the effectiveness of domestic policies. True though this concern is, it applies to economic openness in general; that is, it encompasses the openness of the trade and the current accounts as well. Therefore, this would be an argument against opening the economy (which would carry hardly any support as a general economic policy proposition) and not against capital account liberalization as such.[10]

Traditional *benefits of capital account liberalization*, in turn, include the increase in welfare made possible by the availability of foreign savings to supplement the domestic resource base, which makes feasible a larger capital stock and places the economy on a potentially higher growth path than otherwise. From another perspective, free trade in capital (e.g., though international borrowing and lending flows) can help reduce the costs of the intertemporal misalignments that periodically arise between the patterns of production and consumption. Another benefit to be derived from freedom in capital transactions is that by allowing for trade in risk assets, the sharing and diversification of risks that otherwise would not be possible become feasible.

In essence, the analysis of the costs and benefits of capital account liberalization does not differ much from traditional views of the advantages and disadvantages of free trade in general. Both have to do with the pros and cons of closed versus open systems. *Closed systems,* other things being equal, will neither suffer from (import) external shocks nor will they disseminate (export) the consequences of internal shocks. *Open systems,* in contrast, will be influenced by (import) external shocks and they will disseminate (export) the effects of their domestic shocks.

Capital controls, by tending to close economies, act to insulate them within the system, for better or for worse. As is the case with all types of controls, the effectiveness of those used to contain capital flows will erode over time. Yet, for a time at least, they can inhibit certain types of external financial transactions, limit access to international markets, restrict domestic financial market competition and, most likely, discourage the repatriation of flight capital. In this manner, capital controls can introduce distortions and give rise to inefficiencies in the domestic financial system that will impair the competitiveness of the economy at large. Thus, although they are often advocated as a protective shield, capital controls can instead increase an economy's vulnerability to financial and other economic shocks.

The presence of capital controls can add further distortions if they enable a government to put off addressing prevailing sources of imbalance and to continue inappropriate economic policies. In these circumstances, it will take controls of increasing restrictiveness to offset the erosion of their effectiveness and allow for the maintenance of the causes of imbalance and for the delay in appropriate policy action. Apart from the costs that will likely arise from attempts to capture the "rents" to which capital controls give rise, there is also the risk of *moral hazard* that the efforts to evade capital controls can create for other areas of economic activity. Thus, the use of capital controls to tax capital transactions may not only encourage flight of resources abroad but can also provide incentives to engage in other unofficial activities, a moral hazard risk that should not be underestimated.

Capital Flows and Macroeconomic Policy

The possibility alluded to above of avoiding taxes when capital controls are lifted demonstrates the immediate impact of capital account openness on the effectiveness of government policies. Again, this is no more and no less than a specific manifestation of the general principle that it is easier to influence a closed system by policy or by other internal means than it is to affect an open environment. Therefore, clearly the *ability to tax* arbitrarily is very much limited by the dismantling of capital controls. This may be seen (and it has often been described) as a reduction in the effectiveness of *fiscal policy* brought about by the liberalization of capital flows. But there is no such reduction in fiscal policy *efficiency*, a more important consideration, because efficiency is bound to increase with the elimination of the distortions caused by capital controls. Moreover, it need not be true with regard to fiscal policy *effectiveness* either: first, the very tendency (often successful) to circumvent the controls will make the ability to tax in the presence of capital restrictions more apparent than real; second, the immediate effectiveness of controls (actually, it should be the effectiveness of the introduction and progressive tightening of such controls) should be distinguished from their longer-term effectiveness, which undoubtedly will shrink with the erosion of the ability of controls to insulate the economy.

The relationships that are most often discussed are those between capital movements and monetary and exchange rate policies. A well-known argument that links the three together is often brought up in discussions of the advantages and disadvantages of different exchange rate regimes. The point is frequently made that with a freely floating exchange rate, the independence and effectiveness of domestic monetary policy can be maintained even in the presence of an open capital account. The flip side of this argument is that with a fixed exchange rate, the independence and effectiveness of domestic monetary policy can only be preserved by the establishment of capital controls.

Both arguments, however, are spurious, except in the short run. Under flexible exchange rates, the independence and effectiveness of domestic monetary policy with an open capital account can only be maintained if the monetary policy stance is broadly compatible with that prevailing abroad. Monetary policy, like other domestic policies in general, competes in the world economy so that there will be a tendency for resources to flow toward the countries where the best quality monetary management is in effect. This tendency is contained by the freely floating exchange rate since this rate will move (depreciate) to the extent necessary to eliminate the incentive for resources to flow abroad. In essence, then, this is equivalent to the argument—also often made—that with a flexible exchange rate a national economy can choose its own inflation rate. But this can only be true temporarily, as resources will tend to flow toward stable environments rather than stay in settings where the efforts to maintain stability are characterized by attempts to try to offset one instability (that in the price level) with another (that in the exchange rate).

Similarly, in the case of fixed exchange rates, it is misleading to argue that capital controls can preserve the independence and effectiveness of monetary policy. As was pointed out above, monetary policies compete internationally; resources will tend to move toward the domain of the best quality policies, and the situation here is one of containing that tendency by means of quantity restrictions (capital controls), rather than by means of price adjustments (flexible exchange rates). In effect, an analogous argument can be made that the attainment of monetary autonomy by capital controls is equivalent to saying that by the introduction of capital controls a country can choose its own inflation rate. Other than in the short run, the argument is indeed spurious; controls can only attempt to contain the tendency for resources to flow out, but they will not eliminate it. In the process, their effectiveness will be eroded, and with it the independence of monetary policy and the possibility of choosing a national inflation rate that differs significantly from that prevailing abroad. This sequence of events can be slowed down, though not stopped, by progressively tighter controls. In general, however, the tendency will be for resources to move toward stable environments and to escape from those where the consequences of price instability are temporarily contained by capital controls.

The basic argument to be made is that domestic monetary policies are endogenous to domestic as well as foreign economic market forces. Attempts to circumvent these forces, effective though they may initially be, can only be doomed to eventual failure. All the arguments against the use of quantitative restrictions in the market for goods and services and on the consequent international trade flows apply just as strongly in the context of the capital market and international capital movements.

With the globalization of international capital markets following the dismantling of national capital controls, a phenomenon observed in many economies is that capital inflows from abroad can threaten domestic inflation objectives (another way of expressing the loss of monetary independence) or can impair the economy's competitiveness (thus showing the link between capital flows and exchange rate developments). The dilemma posed by capital inflows is that action taken to meet inflation objectives (in particular, letting the exchange rate appreciate rather than allowing the domestic monetary expansion that would result from the inflows of capital in the absence of exchange rate adjustments) will endanger competitiveness, and that protecting competitiveness (by not allowing the exchange rate to appreciate and, thus, accepting the monetary expansion induced by capital inflows) may jeopardize inflation control (and eventually competitiveness as well). In most circumstances, both a measure of inflation control and of competitiveness are typically lost.

Traditional means to resolve the conflict have consisted of attempts to sterilize the capital inflows—at the expense of expansion of the domestic public debt, which tends to keep interest rates high, thus raising fiscal costs and perpetuating inflows in search of attractive yields; adoption of dual exchange rates—which distort the economy and are often circumvented; and efforts to tighten fiscal policy—which is a valid policy option if the scale of the fiscal adjustment and of capital inflows are commensurate, though not otherwise. Over the long haul, besides the maintenance of sound domestic policies, the optimal reaction to capital inflows is to enhance the flexibility of factor and product markets so that exchange rate appreciation can be compensated for by domestic cost and price decreases, thus keeping domestic goods competitive and inflation at bay.

In sum, freedom of capital flows does not eliminate macroeconomic policy independence. Openness of the economy does that. And the pursuit of a flexible exchange rate policy does not restore policy independence. Although it is true that exchange rate flexibility helps to insulate the economy, it will not be sufficient to bring about complete insulation, particularly in the presence of unsustainable domestic policies which provide incentives for resources to flow to more stable settings.

Thus, the perceptions of domestic policy constraints due to capital account opening can only be real in the short term, as a transitory stage. And such perceptions do not pertain exclusively to capital controls. They are applicable to all types of controls, be they on flow (trade) or stock (capital) variables or of domestic or foreign origin. Much though capital controls can be justified as instruments to deal with specific circumstances or defended on country-case grounds, the fundamental fact remains that controls are an inefficient way to guide economic behavior or enhance policy effectiveness.

Systemic Considerations

Many of the observations made so far can be placed in a systemic setting in order to provide the rationale for updating the international code of conduct to reflect the reality of the world economic environment. The discussion below will be conducted from the standpoint of the International Monetary Fund in its capacity as guardian of the code of conduct.

Much progress has been made in the last half century toward trade and current account openness, perhaps the central challenge that the world economy confronted in the wake of World War II. A main function of the IMF was to supervise countries' observance of constraints on national policies (e.g., such as the proscription on the use of exchange restrictions or of discriminatory practices) meant to maintain this openness. To a large extent, its success laid the foundations for the emergence of capital flows on an increasing scale which only came to reinforce the commitment to an open and globally integrated system. From the mid-1970s on, the capital accounts rose in prominence and eventually came to surpass the current accounts in importance.[11] And yet, despite these broad-ranging developments and the onset and resolution of an international debt crisis, the international code of conduct has remained unchanged with respect to the norms governing capital flows.

By the mid-1990s, the predominance of capital movements had become a permanent feature of the world economic setting; in fact, it can well be said that capital flows constitute an important part of its structure. And those movements took off in the period of flexible exchange rate arrangements that succeeded the Bretton Woods order. It could be argued that such flexibility rendered redundant the need for capital (or any other external) controls, just as it was often argued that freely floating exchange rates reduced the need for international reserves. Neither argument conformed to reality, though: despite exchange rate flexibility, international reserves continued to be needed and capital controls remained in place in many countries, although in a growing number of cases those controls became less predominant. In the process, a state of world economic affairs that linked exchange rates and exchange rate management closely with trade and current account flows moved to a setting where exchange rates and exchange rate management—because of the influence of capital flows and the capital account —became even more closely related to monetary policies and to monetary conditions in countries' economies. Experience with high capital mobility has shown that the independence of monetary policy, in particular, and of domestic economic management, in general, is indeed more apparent than real. A consequence of this development is the need for consistent policies across countries as a condition for orderly economic developments. These considerations in effect stress the increasing futility of attempts at pursuing national objectives at the expense of international aims.

Looking at the international economy as a whole, there are grounds to argue for capital account convertibility as a code of conduct aim of equivalent importance to that of current account convertibility. Capital controls and other restrictions on international capital transactions should receive treatment similar to that given to current account restrictions. The separate treatment given so far to these two types of restrictions carries no weight in logic. But at present neither does it carry weight in practice, as capital flows across nations on an increasing scale and with growing freedom. As a result, where they remain, capital controls have become far less effective than they would be in a setting characterized by a network of widespread constraints on the movement of assets across national borders. As was the case with current account liberalization during Bretton Woods, the establishment of freedom for capital transactions represents a key challenge for the membership of the International Monetary Fund. But, in practice, the challenge has already been substantially met by world economic developments.

Concluding Remarks

There is a consensus that, other things being equal, capital account openness is preferable to capital controls. The case for those controls is typically based on second-best reasoning, and it has often been accompanied by discussions of the *preconditions* that an economy should satisfy before considering external financial liberalization. These conditions typically include, besides a stock of foreign reserves, the establishment of macroeconomic stability at a realistic rate of exchange. An important element of the setting, of course, is a sustainable fiscal position. And it is desirable to have in addition a liberal domestic financial system and one already endowed with a sound safety net to withstand the inroads of foreign competition. But as in many other areas of economics, waiting for these conditions to materialize before proceeding to liberalize capital movements may prove the best recipe for permanent capital controls. Just as plausible is the opposite argument: that the capital account should be opened with no prior conditions. It can be argued that an open capital account will constrain domestic policies to the extent necessary to bring balance and stability to the economy. On this reasoning, a stable macroeconomy, rather than being a precondition for liberalization of capital transactions, can also be seen as a result of capital account convertibility. Similar arguments can be made with regard to the exchange rate—open capital flows will bring about a realistic exchange rate rather than require it ex ante; and the same reasoning applies to the need for domestic financial liberalization, which can also be seen as an outcome of, rather than a prerequisite for, external financial opening. Clearly, in the extreme, neither of these positions will likely apply to any actual country's economy. Neither should the opening of the capital account wait until all desirable conditions are in place, because such an event is unlikely to occur. Nor should it proceed in the absence of a minimum of favorable domestic economic conditions. Balance between these two extremes is necessary. Such balance means that capital account liberalization should be undertaken in less than optimal domestic economic conditions, but not under circumstances so far away from optimality that the credibility of the decision to open the economy to international financial transactions is so impaired that it cannot be sustained.

Another pragmatic consideration often raised in discussions of capital account liberalization concerns the *sequence* of balance of payments opening; that is, whether current account opening should precede or follow liberalization of the capital account.[12] Many economists favor opening the current account first for a variety of reasons including, in particular, the different speeds of adjustment in the market for goods and services and in that for capital; the former is perceived as slower and, therefore, in need of lead time in its opening to the external environment. But there does not seem to be any *a priori* reason why the two accounts could not be opened up simultaneously, if only because the very presence of capital controls can be an obstacle to current account liberalization. Although there is no categorical answer to the issue of sequencing—which, in any event, is influenced by the initial conditions and structure of individual economies—it is plausible to argue for simultaneous rather than sequential liberalization, if accompanied by credible, sound domestic economic policies in a stable external environment.

A related issue to the sequence of liberalization is that of its *speed*, on which arguments can be grouped as favoring either a gradual or a rapid approach. Here again, no single, unconditional answer can be given. But the advantages and disadvantages of each approach warrant gauging. Gradual opening softens the inroads of external competition and provides leeway for domestic preparation to confront that competition. But precisely by giving time to adjust, there is no guarantee that the time will be used to prepare for external competition as opposed to continuing to exploit the opportunities of a closed or partially closed economy. If gradual opening encourages delays in adjustment, its costs will not fall below those from a rapid liberalization and it will not benefit from the latter's advantages. These advantages are the transparent signals that rapid opening of the economy conveys to economic agents and the consequent total absence of leeway for delays in behavioral adjustments to external competition.

It is generally agreed that efficiency criteria argue for completely free exchange systems, with appropriate safeguards, of course. But there are also pragmatic considerations for the establishment of full currency convertibility. These considerations include the desirability of strengthening the role of market forces as opposed to administrative controls; the need to encourage international resource flows; and the need to supplement domestic financial market liberalization and deregulation. In conclusion, economic logic advocates the dismantling of capital controls; developments in the world economy make them undesirable and ineffective; and a strong case can be made in support of rapid and decisive liberalization of capital transactions. All these considerations point strongly to a code of conduct that eschews resort to capital controls as an acceptable course of action for economic policy.

Notes

The views expressed in this paper are mine and should not be attributed to the International Monetary Fund. A different version of this paper was presented at an International Conference on "Money and Finance in the Open Economy" sponsored by the Institute of Economic Research of Korea University and the Bank of Korea, held in Seoul on November 6–7, 1992; see Guitián (1995). The general issue of international capital flows and the particular subject of capital account liberalization have been extensively studied in the International Monetary Fund. In the preparation of this paper I have relied heavily on the Fund's most recent studies, including International Monetary Fund (1991), Mathieson and Rojas-Suárez (1993), and Calvo, Leiderman and Reinhart (1993).

1. In particular, the *Articles of Agreement* of the International Monetary Fund, which contain such code of conduct, prescribe that "Members may exercise such controls as are necessary to regulate international capital movements, but no member may exercise these controls in a manner which restricts payments for current transactions or which will unduly delay transfers of funds in settlements of commitments, except as provided in Article VIII, Section 3(b) and in Article XIV, Section 2" (Article VI, Section 3).

2. See Article VIII of the *Articles of Agreement* in the International Monetary

Fund (1992). It must be pointed out, in this context, that in its definition of current account transactions the *Articles of Agreement* include some capital account items (see Article XXX of the *Articles of Agreement*). International capital flows are also a subject of interest for the Organization of Economic Cooperation and Development (OECD), as made evident by the adoption of the *Code of Liberalization of Current Invisible Transactions* and the *Code of Liberalization of Capital* soon after the organization's establishment: see Fischer and Reisen (1992).

3. The Bretton Woods period encompasses the years during which the international economy operated under a fixed exchange rate regime, the par value system adopted at the Bretton Woods conference that established the World Bank and the International Monetary Fund. See Horsefield (1969), de Vries (1976), and Guitián (1992a).

4. For an exposition of issues related to currency convertibility, see Polak (1991), Williamson (1991), Guitián (1992b, 1995), and Greene and Isard (1991).

5. This period has been examined *in extenso* by de Vries (1985). The points made in the text have been discussed in more detail in Guitián (1992c), where issues related to the international debt crisis, its origins and resolution are also studied.

6. See, for example, Mathieson and Rojas-Suárez (1993), Guitián (1993) and the International Monetary Fund (1991).

7. An abundant literature exists on the subject of the international debt crisis. A list of sources can be found in "The International Debt Crisis: What Have we Learned?" in Guitián (1992c); see also Guitián (1992d). For the general evolution of international capital flows over the last two decades, see International Monetary Fund (1991).

8. For further discussion of the evaluation of yield differentials, see International Monetary Fund (1991) and Frankel (1991).

9. For an excellent exposition of the importance of this shift in economic policy from reliance on government guidance toward respect for market forces, see Polak (1991).

10. An extensive discussion of the costs and benefits of liberalization of the capital account is found in Hanson (1992).

11. A detailed examination of these capital account developments will be found in Goldstein, Mathieson and Lane, "Determinants and Systemic Consequences of International Capital Flows," in International Monetary Fund (1991).

12. An excellent discussion of the various issues involved in the decision to liberalize an economy and of the sequence in which it should be undertaken will be found in McKinnon (1991).

References

Calvo, Guillermo A., Leonardo Leiderman and Carmen M. Reinhart. 1993. "Capital Inflows and Real Exchange Rate Appreciation in Latin America: The Role of External Factors." *IMF Staff Papers* 40(1): 108–51.

de Vries, Margaret Garritsen. 1976. *The International Monetary Fund, 1966–1971: The System Under Stress.* Washington: International Monetary Fund.

———. 1985. *The International Monetary Fund, 1972–1978: Cooperation on Trial.* Washington: International Monetary Fund.

Fischer, Bernhard, and Helmut Reisen. 1992. *Towards Capital Account Convertibility*. OECD Development Centre, Policy Brief No. 4. Paris: Organization for Economic Cooperation and Development.

Frankel, Jeffrey A. 1991. "Quantifying International Capital Mobility in the 1980s," in Douglas Bernheim and John B. Shoven, eds., *National Saving and Economic Performance*. Pp. 56–77. Chicago: University of Chicago Press.

Greene, Joshua E., and Peter Isard. 1991. "Currency Convertibility and the Transformation of Centrally Planned Economies." *IMF Occasional Paper* No. 81. Washington: International Monetary Fund.

Guitián, Manuel. 1995. "Capital Account Liberalization: Bringing Policy in Line with Reality," in Sebastian Edwards, ed., *Capital Controls, Exchange Rates and Monetary Policy in the World Economy*. Pp. 71–90. Cambridge: Cambridge University Press.

———. 1993. "An Old-Fashioned Vision of Monetary Policy for an Emerging Europe," in *The Monetary Future of Europe*. Pp. 1–19. London: Centre for Economic Policy Research.

———. 1992a. "The Unique Nature of the Responsibilities of the International Monetary Fund." *IMF Pamphlet Series* No. 46. Washington: International Monetary Fund.

———. 1992b. "Monetary and Exchange Rate Policies for Stabilization and Reform." Paper presented to a seminar on *The Transition and Adjustment* at the Joint Vienna Institute on October 6, 1992.

———. 1992c. "Rules and Discretion in International Economic Policy." *IMF Occasional Paper* No. 97. Washington: International Monetary Fund.

———. 1992d. "Remarks on the Debt Crisis," in Paul A. Volcker and Toyoo Gyohten, eds., *Changing Fortunes: The World's Money and the Decline of American Supremacy*. Pp. 318–22. New York: Times Books.

Hanson, James A. 1992. "Opening the Capital Account: A Survey of Issues and Results." *Policy Research Working Papers*, WPS 901. Washington: World Bank.

Horsefield, J. Keith, ed. 1969. *The International Monetary Fund, 1945-65: Twenty Years of International Monetary Cooperation*. Washington: International Monetary Fund.

International Monetary Fund. 1991. "Determinants and Systemic Consequences of International Capital Flows." *IMF Occasional Paper* No. 77. Washington: International Monetary Fund.

———. 1992. *Articles of Agreement*. Washington: International Monetary Fund.

Mathieson, Donald J., and Liliana Rojas-Suárez. 1993. "Liberalization of the Capital Account: Experiences and Issues." *IMF Occasional Paper* No. 103. Washington: International Monetary Fund, June.

McKinnon, Ronald I. 1991. *The Order of Economic Liberalization*. Baltimore: Johns Hopkins University Press.

Polak, Jacques J. 1991. "Convertibility: An Indispensable Element in the Transition Process in Eastern Europe," in John Williamson, ed., *Currency Convertibility in Eastern Europe*. Pp. 21–30. Washington: Institute for International Economics.

Williamson, John, ed. 1991. *Currency Convertibility in Eastern Europe*. Washington: Institute for International Economics.

3

Preconditions for Liberalization of Capital Flows: A Review and Interpretation

Clas Wihlborg and Kalman Dezseri

Introduction

The literature on currency convertibility and, in particular, on the liberalization of capital account transactions has become voluminous during the last decade. One reason for the strong interest in convertibility is the increasing market orientation of economic policy in many developing countries. The dramatic shift from central planning towards market economies in Eastern Europe has also contributed.

There are several excellent reviews of the literature on the pros and cons of capital account convertibility.[1] Recent literature puts a strong emphasis on the sequencing of capital account liberalization relative to current account liberalization, financial sector liberalization, and macroeconomic stabilization. Much of the earlier literature was concerned with the role of capital flows for macroeconomic stabilization or with costs and benefits of foreign direct investments.

There is now wide-spread agreement among economists that full convertibility is desirable in developing countries, as well as in industrialized countries. Disagreements remain, however, on the necessary and sufficient conditions for a country to benefit from the process of capital account liberalization given imperfections in markets and concern with other policy objectives than economic efficiency.

In this chapter we discuss how the analysis of sequencing of liberalization and the arguments for limited convertibility depend either on market failures in the conventional sense, or policy failures in the sense that for political reasons authorities are unable to deal with an economic problem using the instrument with the least costs in terms of other policy objectives. Several of the common arguments for capital controls are questioned here on the grounds that they depend on assumptions about policy and market failures being exogenous. Relaxing capital controls may actually provide policymakers with incentives to address market failures directly. We will also argue that a capital control policy requires the fine-tuning of the controls for desired objectives to be achieved.

To put the distinction between policy and market failures into perspective, we compare analyses of the costs and benefits of capital controls with analyses of the costs and benefits of commercial policy.[2] The analogy between commercial policy and capital controls is not perfect, however. Analyses of commercial policy tend to consider efficiency and welfare issues, whereas optimality criteria are less well defined in macroeconomic analysis. Capital controls play a large role in analyses of macroeconomic policy and adjustment, and expectations formation and risk are important considerations in the analysis of capital account transactions.[3] Assumptions with respect to these concepts are often based on the analyst's prior beliefs.

In the next section we review commonly discussed preconditions for liberalization of capital account transactions and relate them to policy and market failures. The third section focuses on policy failure arguments for capital controls, while market failure arguments are discussed in the fourth section. In the fifth section external capital flow surges are discussed, and the final section presents our conclusions.

Preconditions for Capital Account Liberalization

Several reviews of arguments for and against capital account liberalization and of the proper place for such liberalization in a sequence of reforms conclude with a list of preconditions for the liberalization of inflows, outflows or both. Hanson (1995) and Mathieson and Rojas-Suárez (1992) include the following preconditions:

1. A stable macroeconomy characterized (at least) by the absence of high and unstable inflation according to Hanson (1995). In the view of Mathieson and Rojas-Suárez (1992), a stable macroeconomy requires small differences in financial market conditions relative to the world, wage and price flexibility, and fiscal discipline.
2. Domestic financial controls on interest rates and portfolio allocation are abolished; also, domestic banks should have a "sound" portfolio

according to Hanson (1995). In the view of Mathieson and Rojas-Suárez (1992), the corresponding preconditions are flexible interest rates, restructured and recapitalized financial institutions, and a reduction in the safety net accorded these institutions.

Williamson (1992) suggests that liberalization should be subject to more restrictive conditions, and distinguishes between preconditions for the liberalization of capital inflows and outflows. As preconditions for the liberalization of inflows, he adds the following considerations to those relating to domestic financial liberalization noted above:

3. Structural adjustment programs should be in place with nontraditional export industries firmly established.
4. The current account should be liberalized before the capital account.
5. Fiscal discipline should be established.

Condition 1 above (regarding macroeconomic stability in Hanson's 1995 terminology) refers primarily to the liberalization of capital outflows. Williamson's list of preconditions for capital outflow liberalization includes:

6. A policy regime that investors regards as permanent.
7. The ability to manage demand by a measure of fiscal flexibility.
8. The existence of arrangements to limit the erosion of the tax base.

Conditions 6 and 7 can be seen as specific requirements for a stable macroeconomy. Condition 8 is based on concerns that outflows may reduce the inflation tax base.

Some of the above mentioned preconditions for liberalization of both capital outflows and inflows are also thought to be causes of surges in capital inflows in developing countries and, therefore, grounds for imposing inflow regulation. Schadler *et al.* (1993) review recent experiences of such surges. They conclude that successful structural reform, the achievement of fiscal discipline, and credible tightening of domestic credit policies have been important causes of rapid and large capital inflows. These causes of inflows are "internal" in the terminology of Calvo *et al.* (1993). "External" causes contributing to surges in inflows, according to Schadler *et al.*, are the lowering of foreign interest rates and bandwagon effects.

The similarity between these preconditions for capital account liberalization and causes of surges of capital inflows raises questions about cause and effect in the analysis of capital flows. The following observations summarize overlaps between preconditions and causes, and areas of disagreement:

OBSERVATION 1. *Successful structural adjustment and fiscal discipline are considered both preconditions for liberalization of inflows and causes of surges of inflows.*

OBSERVATION 2. *Successful macroeconomic stabilization is considered a precondition for liberalization of outflows, as well as a cause of capital inflows.*

OBSERVATION 3. *There is disagreement about the sequencing of capital account liberalization relative to current account liberalization and structural reform programs.*

OBSERVATION 4. *There is general agreement that the liberalization of financial markets and well-functioning domestic financial institutions are preconditions for capital account liberalization.*

OBSERVATION 5. *There is disagreement whether external "shocks" to capital flows should be controlled by means of capital controls.*

Observations 1 and 2 refer primarily to the general policy environment within a country and the progress of market-oriented micro and macro policies. Observations 3 and 4 refer to the potential roles of failures in domestic goods, factor, and financial markets for the allocational effects of capital flows. Observation 5, finally, relates to disagreements about the "rationality" of participants in international financial markets.

In the following, we discuss first the "success" of market-oriented policies as arguments for and against capital account liberalization. We then examine the role of market failures and, finally, conditions in the external environment and their role in capital account liberalization.

The Policy Environment

Capital flows are to a large extent driven by relative expected returns and risks on real and financial investments in various countries. Expected returns are often low and risks high in countries with high and variable inflation rates. One reason is that these conditions lead to expectations of restrictive macroeconomic policies. Another is that the same conditions are often caused by rigid factor markets and an inefficient use of available resources. In these countries return and risk considerations may lead to capital flight, a decrease in the amount of domestic and foreign savings available for real investments, and an erosion of the inflation tax base.[4]

It is not obvious that capital outflows are welfare reducing under conditions of macroeconomic mismanagement and poorly functioning markets for goods and factors of production. Individuals are able to protect the value of their wealth by investing in environments where the risk-adjusted expected return is higher. Governments conducting policies inducing capital outflows are obviously reluctant to accept that scarce savings are invested abroad because of their policies. Thus, they impose exchange controls or they delay liberalization of controls.

The economic argument against capital flow liberalization in an inflationary and rigid environment rests either on an assumption that policy authorities cannot substitute other taxes for an inflation tax or that the policy stance of the government with respect to inflation and market rigidities is exogenous and unresponsive to events in markets. In both cases there is an assumption about policy failure.

Generally, governments conducting nonmarket-oriented policies causing rigidity in factor and product markets, and thus suffering capital flight, are simply unwilling on ideological grounds to conduct market-oriented policies. Such governments are reluctant to subject themselves to market forces that make it more costly to conduct their desired policies. Therefore, capital outflow controls are often a logical consequence of an ideological policy stance. There is, however, no reason for economists to accept such government arguments for capital controls as a demonstration of the positive welfare effects of controls.

Consider next a more interesting situation, when a market-oriented government favoring liberalization of factor and product markets, and a restrictive monetary policy, has come to power inheriting an economy characterized by inflation, rigid factor and product markets, and a low rate of return or high risk on investments. The new government conducts more restrictive monetary and fiscal policies and initiates structural reforms. The "policy failure" mentioned above is removed. Should the new government delay capital account liberalization until inflation has come down and structural reforms have had a substantial effect? According to the preconditions for liberalization reviewed in the previous section, a delay is desirable until reforms have had intended effects, the banking sector has been liberalized, and fiscal policy has demonstratively become a flexible policy instrument.

It is useful to distinguish between a situation in which the policies of the new government are not credible, on the one hand, and one in which reforms are credible, on the other. In the first case, lack of credibility could be the result of a high probability that the government will not succeed in reforming the economy before being voted out of office. In this situation, real and financial investors will continue to favor foreign assets. A monetary contraction will push real interest rates to high levels. A premium is required on financial securities to compensate for the lack of credibility of anti-inflation policies and a risk premium is required on real investments for the same reason.

When its credibility is low, the market-oriented government would benefit from capital inflows, and capital outflows would increase the costs of the reform program. Net capital inflows would reduce the need for high real interest rates to compensate for the government's lack of credibility, but uncertainty about future policies is a disincentive for inflows.

In the second case, the new government's market-oriented reforms are credible. Then real interest rates increase less and only a smaller risk premium on real investments is required. As in the preceding scenario, capital inflows are potentially beneficial, and they reduce the costs of adjustment to a new policy stance. Capital inflows are much more likely in this scenario. The inflows can even become too large, causing a real appreciation in a situation when a real depreciation is desirable for the traded goods sector. This sector needs to draw (still too immobile) factors of production from unproductive uses. This situation is described by, for example, Dornbusch (1983), Edwards and Edwards (1987), and Frenkel (1983). The possibility of a real appreciation provides the argument for macroeconomic stabilization and structural adjustment to be completed, and not just initiated, as preconditions for the liberalization of capital inflows.

The discussion so far provides an argument for delaying the liberalization of capital outflows when market-oriented reform and macroeconomic stabilization policies lack credibility, and for delaying the liberalization of capital inflows until reforms have had substantial success, even when reforms are credible. It seems therefore that "optimizing" policies relative to capital account liberalization requires "fine tuning" based on general perceptions about credibility. Such fine tuning is complicated by the possibility that the credibility of reforms could be endogenous relative to policies with respect to capital controls, in particular with respect to capital outflows.

What is the role of policy and market failures in the arguments for delays in liberalization of capital inflows and outflows? The above argument for delay in the liberalization of outflows is based on lack of credibility of reform policies. In other words, it is the possibility of future "policy failures" that induce outflows and these outflows could raise the costs of reform policies.

The arguments for delays in the liberalization of capital inflows, however, depend on a combination of market and policy failures. One type of relevant market failure is rigidity in factor and goods markets, perhaps caused by policies of previous nonmarket-oriented governments. This rigidity implies that the reforming economy's ability to absorb real investments in productive sectors is limited. A substantial real depreciation is therefore required to induce mobility to those sectors, but a surge in capital inflows causes a real appreciation, delaying the adjustment. Edwards and Edwards (1987) refer to this mechanism in the Chilean experience of the late 1970s, and Schadler *et al.* (1993) refer to similar experiences in Latin America during the 1980s.

Additional policy or market failures are required for the argument against liberalization of capital inflows to carry weight. One reason is that the real appreciation caused by a surge in inflows could be reduced by allowing the real interest rate to fall or to increase less; such reductions might be made without risking inflation if the reform policies are credible. A reduced real interest rate lowers the cost of capital for firms, increases the willingness to invest, and therefore increases the absorption of capital inflows. The reduction in the real interest rate, which could reduce pressure on the real exchange rate to appreciate, may be hindered by an inflexible fiscal policy, however.

Another question that can be raised is why capital inflows would be so large as to exceed an amount that can be used productively in the new policy environment. One possibility is that there are domestic financial market failures. This would explain why domestic financial sector reforms are considered a precondition for the liberalization of inflows as noted in the previous section. De la Cuadra and Valdés (1992) argue that the Chilean banking system seriously misallocated financial resources made available by capital inflows, because bank managers felt their investments were implicitly guaranteed by the government.

Bandwagon effects and bubbles in financial markets causing asset price inflation have also been pointed to as causes of misallocation of financial resources.[5] In this explanation, capital flows are based on other considerations than fundamental economic developments. We consider such capital flows further below.

In conclusion, a government initiating market reforms and a macroeconomic stabilization program could face either a problem of insufficient capital inflows because of a lack of credibility or a problem of misallocated or excessive capital inflows. Misallocated flows would be caused by failures in markets for factors of production and financial resources or by failures in the fiscal policy response to high real interest rates. In general, combinations of these failures are required to argue for delays in capital account liberalization.

Although it is easy to find theoretical arguments favoring delays in the liberalization of the capital account, it is less clear whether a government in the reform process should restrict inflows and outflows. Without freedom of capital flows, the government may not get clear signals about the degree to which its reform policies are considered credible by the market. It is possible that its credibility is neither so low as to induce outflows nor so high as to induce surges of inflows. Capital controls are not policy instruments well suited for fine tuning in response to variations in the credibility of government policies. Furthermore, a combination of policy failures must be present to make the case for capital controls.

Market Failures and the Sequencing of Reforms

In the previous section two market failure arguments were presented for delaying the liberalization of capital inflows in the presence of policy failures. In both cases, the economy was in the initial stages of market-oriented reforms and in need of substantial reallocation of resources to the tradables sector. In one case, the argument was that lingering rigidities in factor and product markets could force a large real appreciation in response to a surge in capital inflows. In the second case, failures in the financial sector allocation of credits were the cause of a misallocation of capital inflows. Neither argument implies that the optimum level of capital inflow is zero, or the amount that gets around inflow controls is zero. In the case where there are rigidities in factor and product markets, inflows that correspond to the ability of the economy to use the inflows productively are desirable; similarly, an imperfect financial sector does not misallocate all capital inflows. Thus, under both these market failure arguments, an optimal amount of capital inflows requires fine tuning of capital controls. How this optimum is going to be achieved is not discussed in the literature.

Market failure arguments for limiting capital inflows are, as noted, analogous to the basic proposition in the theory of commercial policy that tariffs can be welfare increasing in the presence of distortions in factor and goods markets. A second proposition in this branch of international trade theory is that trade policy is (almost) never the first-best policy response to market failures. The first-best response is directed at the particular market where failures occur. Thus, the argument for a trade policy response to market failures requires both market failure and a policy failure that makes the first-best policy politically infeasible. Analogous arguments apply on policies limiting capital inflows. For example, the first-best response to rigidities in factor markets is measures reducing those rigidities and, if this is not possible, subsidies to the mobility of factors of production. If policy failures prevent these responses, then a case for protectionism can be built.

The debate over the sequencing of liberalization of the current and capital accounts of the balance of payments is also very much based on market failures. For example, Krueger (1984) argues that capital account transactions should be liberalized last because capital flows, like all financial market transactions, depend on the present value of distorted prices, if the current account is not already liberalized. If there are costs of reallocating the capital stock after the liberalization of the current account, then the investments taking place at distorted prices will reduce future investments at non-distorted prices. One weakness of this argument is that it presumes that the current account liberalization program is not anticipated. If it were, the expected sequence of liberalization of prices and costs of reallocation of physical capital would be incorporated in present value calculations. Thus, it seems that Krueger's reasoning does not apply to a credible liberalization process.

Gangopadhyay and Wadhwa (1994) present another case where early capital account liberalization is welfare decreasing. They assume that a fixed share of imported inputs is required in production. The benefits of current account liberalization in this case are obvious. Capital account liberalization alone, however, leads to depreciation and an increase in the cost of imported inputs.

Other economists favoring the delay of capital account liberalization until the adjustment to low tariffs has been completed are McKinnon (1991), Frenkel (1982, 1983), Edwards (1984), and Edwards and Wijnbergen (1986). Their arguments are the same as those presented above for delays until structural adjustment is completed.

There exist also arguments in the literature favoring speedy capital account liberalization. For example, Little, Scitovsky and Scott (1970, Ch. 10), Michaely (1986) and Krueger (1984) note that the adjustment to the decline of import-competing industries can be smoothed by capital inflows financing investments in expanding sectors. This argument underscores the point made above, that optimal policy with respect to the sequencing of liberalization requires fine tuning of capital controls.

External Causes of Surges in Capital Inflows

Schadler *et al.* (1993) note that a fall in foreign interest rates in combination with bandwagon effects may be the cause of surges in inflows. Bandwagon effects are essentially market failures implying that participants in international financial markets do not act solely on expectations about fundamental causes of and reasons for capital flows. It is hard to evaluate the importance of bandwagon effects and different types of irrationality that some analysts detect in various incidents. The capital outflows that hit the Mexican economy and other Latin American countries in connection with the Mexican peso crisis in the fall of 1994 seem to many observers to be excessive and caused by a nervous "flight to quality" without corresponding shifts in fundamentals. Such capital flows are obviously damaging to an economy, and welfare would be increased if capital controls hindered them. The problem is to devise a set of capital controls that discriminates between "bad" and "good" capital flows. Recall that analysts at the time disagreed about Mexican fundamentals. Views are now colored by the relative success of the stabilization program Mexico imposed.

A fall in the world interest rate could cause a surge in capital inflows to an economy with high real interest rates. It is hard to see why such inflows, allowing a country to reduce real interest rates, would be damaging unless a "policy failure" makes the high real interest rate unchangeable.

A third external cause of capital inflows has been mentioned in the Baltic states. Political instability in Russia in combination with a substantial demand for the laundering of money seems to be the cause of large capital flows into the Baltic economies. The small size of these economies relative to Russia could make the inflows overwhelming, forcing the countries to appreciate their currencies in real terms. Effectively there has been an increase in the demand for financial services. Resources must then shift into this sector from traditional producing sectors. The appreciation helps induce this resource transfer. The policy problem is really one of a reluctance to accept the activities in the expanding sector. The appropriate response is to strengthen enforcement of law and supervision. The feasibility and effectiveness of such policy measures are questionable, however.

Concluding Remarks

We have reviewed arguments for delaying the liberalization of capital inflows until adjustment to structural programs and tariff reductions is completed, the financial sector has been liberalized and made to allocate credit effectively, fiscal policy has become flexible, and credible macroeconomic stabilization has been achieved. There are obvious merits to each argument for the economic benefits of constraints on capital flows. The main argument against delays in liberalization of capital account transactions is that an optimal strategy for liberalization requires fine-tuning of policies towards these transactions in three respects. First, the nature of the problems caused by capital flows depends on the degree of credibility of a market-oriented reform program and a macroeconomic stabilization program. This credibility is not known at the time a reform program is initiated and credibility may itself depend importantly on policies towards capital flows. Second, the market failures that contribute to costs of capital flows are not complete in the sense that all capital flows have negative effects. Thus, beneficial capital flows must be distinguished from costly capital flows. Third, the policy failures contributing to costs of capital flows may not be exogenous relative to the consequences of capital flows.[6] The information required to determine whether capital flows will be beneficial or costly on net is simply not available, and once a policy has been determined with respect to capital flows it cannot be easily changed in response to actual capital flows.

Another and related argument for not delaying liberalization of capital account transactions is that an optimal policy would probably be one of relaxing controls over time. Politically, the choice is more realistically between liberalizing "too early" and "too late." The literature has not analyzed this tradeoff, but rather tacitly assumed that liberalization can be done at the right time. The political windows of opportunity for liberalization may be short-lived and far between, however.

The policy conclusion that follows from this reasoning is that early liberalization is desirable, if financial market participants are believed to react with reasonable rationality to expected returns and risk, and if these expected returns are based on expectations about economic fundamentals such as future relative prices. Early liberalization of capital account transactions will also enhance the credibility of reform programs. If the financial sector misallocates resources severely, then there could be a reason for limiting the flow of resources to this sector. Speedy reform of the incentive structure in the domestic financial sector is obviously preferable, however.

Notes

1. See, for example, Edwards (1984), Hanson (1995) and Mathieson and Rojas-Suárez (1992).
2. See, for example, Corden (1971).
3. See, for example, Mathieson and Rojas-Suárez (1992) and Sweeney (1996).
4. It is assumed that the reduction in government income through erosion of the inflation tax base is a "bad" thing.
5. A bubble could be caused by a number of investors investing during the early stages of liberalization in the belief that they will be observant enough to get their money out in time if a crisis develops.
6. See Chapter 7 by Wihlborg and Willett in this volume.

References

Corden, W. Max. 1971. *The Theory of Protection.* Oxford: Clarendon Press.

Calvo, Guillermo, Leonardo Leiderman, and Carmen Reinhardt. 1993. "The Capital Inflows Problem: Concepts and Issues." *IMF Paper on Policy Analysis and Assessment*, No. 93/10. Washington, D.C.: International Monetary Fund.

De la Cuadra, Sergio, and Salvador Valdés-Prieto. 1992. "Myths and Facts about Financial Liberalization in Chile; 1974–1983," in Philip L. Brock, ed. , *If Texas Were Chile: A Primer on Banking Reform.* Pp. 11–101. San Francisco: ICS Press.

Dornbusch, Rudiger. 1983. "Flexible Exchange Rates and Interdependence." *IMF Staff Papers*, March: 3–38.

Edwards, Sebastian. 1984. "The Order of Liberalization of the External Sector in Developing Countries." *Princeton Essays in International Finance*, No. 156. Princeton: Princeton University Press.

Edwards, Sebastian, and Alejandra C. Edwards. 1987. *Monetarism and Liberalization: The Chilean Experiment*. Cambridge, Mass.: Ballinger.

Edwards, Sebastian, and Sweder van Wijnbergen. 1986. "The Welfare Effects of Trade and Capital Account Liberalization." *International Economic Review* 27(1): 141–48.

Frenkel, Jacob. 1982. "The Order of Economic Liberalization: A Comment," in Karl Brunner and Allen Meltzer, eds., *Economic Policy in a World of Change*. Pp. 99–102. Carnegie Rochester Conference Series. Amsterdam: North Holland.

____________. 1983. "Panel Discussion on the Southern Cone." *IMF Staff Papers*, March: 164–73.

Gangopadhyay, Shubhashis, and Wilima Wadhwa. 1994. "Dual Markets for Foreign Exchange: Domestic Deficit and Liberalization Policies." Paper presented at the INU Conference on Indian Economic Reforms.

Hanson, James. 1995. "Opening the Capital Account: Costs, Benefits and Sequencing," in Sebastian Edwards, ed., *Capital Controls, Exchange Rates, and Monetary Policy in the World Economy*. Pp. 383–429. Cambridge: Cambridge University Press.

Krueger, Anne. 1984. "Problems of Liberalization," in Arnold Harberger, ed., *World Economic Growth*. Pp. 403–23. San Francisco: ICS Press.

Little, I.M.D, Tibor Scitovsky, and M. Scott. 1970. *Industry and Trade in Some Developing Countries. A Comparative Study*. Oxford: Oxford University Press.

Mathieson, Donald J., and Liliana Rojas-Suárez. 1992. "Liberalization of the Capital Account: Experiences and Issues." *IMF Working Paper*, No. 92/46. Washington, D.C.: International Monetary Fund, June.

McKinnon, Ronald. 1991. *The Order of Economic Liberalization*. Baltimore: Johns Hopkins University Press.

Michaely, Michael. 1986. "The Timing and Sequence of a Trade Liberalization Policy," in Armeane Choksi and Demetris Papaegeorgiou, eds., *Finance Liberalization in Developing Countries*. Pp. 41–59. London: Basil Blackwell.

Schadler, Susan, Maria Carkovic, Adam Bennett, and Ronald Kahn. 1993. *Recent Experiences with Surges in Capital Inflows*. Washington, D.C.: International Monetary Fund, December.

Sweeney, Richard J. 1996. "The Information Costs of Capital Controls." Chapter 4 in this volume.

Williamson, John. 1992. "A Cost Benefit Analysis of Capital Account Liberalization." Paper for OECD conference, *Financial Opening: Developing Country Policy Issues and Experiences*.

4

The Information Costs of Capital Controls

Richard J. Sweeney

Introduction

The 1980s and 1990s have seen an unprecedented wave of countries liberalizing their economies. Liberalizing countries vary widely in the extent to which their economies are pervasively distorted and cut off from free-market price signals, and the degree to which their economies have basic free-market institutions such as a modern commercial law code, generally accepted accounting standards, a modern banking system, well-functioning capital markets, etc. Though the countries differ greatly, all face the issue of the sequencing of liberalization, or which markets to liberalize first. Many countries liberalize their goods markets first, freeing output markets' prices and opening these markets at least partially (and often increasingly) to international competition; in other words, they first liberalize their trade accounts in the balance of payments, a typical pattern of liberalizing Latin American countries (McKinnon 1991). Only later do countries make substantial progress in liberalizing their capital accounts.[1]

The debate about liberalizing capital accounts is mostly at the macro level. Opening capital accounts might increase total investment through increases in inward foreign direct investment.[2] In opposition are two conflicting possibilities. Capital flight might arise from mistrust of the government, resulting perhaps in a fall in aggregate investment. Further, supposing government policies are credible and investment opportunities attractive, massive inward foreign direct investment might drive up the country's real exchange rate enough to cause the country's industries serious harm in international competition.[3] This aggregate focus obscures the allocative role of capital markets in providing signals for choosing among the many competing projects in liberalizing nations.[4]

Some observers note that if a country's capital markets are not open internationally, its interest rates differ from the world's, and that this leads to resource misallocation (just as having output prices different from the world's leads to misallocation). This point is often made in models where the decision maker faces no difficulty in knowing what discount rate to use in investment decisions. This argument misses the point that decision makers must estimate risk-return tradeoffs in evaluating investment projects. Closed capital markets increase the problems of inferring these tradeoffs, and thus lead to capital misallocation.

This chapter makes the case that capital markets should be substantially and progressively liberalized from the beginning rather than waiting until goods market liberalization is well advanced. Though capital controls' effects on aggregate investment are debatable, they likely cause avoidable and potentially serious misallocation of limited capital across competing projects. Further, capital controls reduce the credibility of government promises that international investors will be able to repatriate their funds.

The next section discusses how financial markets generate information that firms can use in setting hurdle rates to evaluate projects. To set hurdle rates, a firm must find the priced systematic risk factors, the premium paid for bearing each type of systematic risk, and the project's betas on each risk factor. In countries integrated with world markets, the firm can free ride on information developed by other decision makers: The firm faces the same risk factors and risk premia as any other, and can also use other decision makers' experience with similar projects to estimate betas. In a country cut off from world markets, the number of systematic risk factors, the risk factors themselves, and the premia on priced factors may differ from international markets; and the experience of firms in other countries may be of little use in estimating betas. The quality of estimates generated from thin, illiquid, new stock markets is substantially lower than from international markets, thus reducing the quality of project choices in liberalizing countries. The argument is not that well-functioning capital markets make no mistakes—they make many each day—rather capital account restrictions likely cause serious enough noise and distortion in financial-market signals that the outcome is significantly worse than it need be.

Following this I show that a liberalizing country with open capital markets may fail to reap the benefits of capital account liberalization if government promises of free repatriation of capital are not fully credible; removing capital controls on residents increases the credibility of government assurances that foreign investors will be allowed to repatriate interest, profits and capital. If government promises to foreign investors are not credible, the country's marginal investors may be domestic residents. In this case, firms have all the problems discussed in the previous section in finding appropriate risk-adjusted hurdle rates. If the marginal investors are international investors, then knowledge developed in international markets can be applied in valuing the country's projects; domestic residents who cannot invest internationally, however, end up holding a project portfolio not structured to take full account of local risk that these residents are prevented from diversifying away.

The following section gives a further discussion of credibility. Government restrictions on domestic residents' capital outflows undermine the credibility of promises of free repatriation of capital and accumulations for foreigners. Further, many Western discussions suggest that capital controls are a useful or even necessary part of liberalizing countries' government policies; this encourages the belief that governments will in a crunch repudiate their promises of free repatriation.

The final section offers a summary and conclusions.

Informational Requirements for Estimating Risk-Adjusted Discount Rates

Open financial markets provide information that can be used to extract appropriate risk-adjusted discount rates to help investors allocate capital among competing uses at the micro level. In this section I discuss how asset markets price securities in terms of risk and expected return. Using this framework, firms can examine securities markets to infer which types of risk concern asset holders and the size of expected rewards that asset holders demand from projects to which they supply capital. Firms can then use this information to decide whether each project they are considering offers a large enough expected return to compensate investors for the risks involved. Thus, information from securities markets allows non-financial firms to make investment decisions that meet market tests in compensating investors for risk. Without this information, firms necessarily often misjudge which risks require compensation for investors and the size of compensation required. Capital goes to poorer uses on average; even capital put to good uses goes too much to some projects, too little to others. Opening capital markets to international competition is the low-cost way of allowing firms to acquire more accurate information on risk. Put another way, capital controls likely prevent a liberalizing country from exploiting its comparative advantages to the full.

An Asset Pricing Model

Consider an asset pricing model based on the Arbitrage Pricing Theory of Ross (1976).[5] Suppose that there are K risk factors and N assets, $K \ll N$. Some observers present evidence that the overall rate of return on the market and interest-rate surprises are among the risk factors (Sweeney and Warga 1986a); other factors for which some observers provide evidence are inflation and term-structure risk (Chen, Roll and Ross 1986; Burmeister, Roll and Ross 1992) and exchange-rate risk. The two key Arbitrage Pricing Theory equations are the generating function

$$R_{it} = \mathrm{E}\, R_{it} + \textstyle\sum_{k=1}^{K} \beta_{kit}\, \delta_{kt} + e_{it}, \qquad i = 1, \ldots, N, \tag{1}$$

and the pricing relationship

$$\mathrm{E}\, R_{it} = r_{ft} + \textstyle\sum_{k=1}^{K} \beta_{kit}\, \lambda_{kt}, \tag{2}$$

where R_{it} is the rate of return on asset i in period t, E the expectation operator as of the start of t, β_{kit} the beta of asset i's return on the kth factor, δ_{kt} the surprise in the kth factor, e_{it} the idiosyncratic error for i, r_{ft} "the" risk-free rate of return,[6] and λ_{kt} the risk premium on the kth factor. From the generating function (1), the return on any asset equals its expected return for that period plus the sum of the asset's betas on economy-wide risk factors times the realizations of the risk factors ($\sum_{k=1}^{K} \beta_{kit}\, \delta_{kt}$), plus an idiosyncratic error. Risk-factor realizations δ_{kt} during period t are surprises conditional on the information set observable by economic agents at the start of t. Thus, surprises in the overall market rate of return or in interest-rate changes or in the inflation rate affect a given firm's actual rate of return, with the effects depending on the generating function slopes (βs).

The pricing relationship (2) says that the expected return on any asset i equals the risk-free rate of return plus the sum across economy-wide risk factors of i's beta on the risk factor k times the premium λ_k on the factor ($\sum_{k=1}^{K} \beta_{kit}\, \lambda_{kt}$).[7] For example, only overall market risk and interest-rate risk might be priced, with premia of perhaps 8 percent for market risk and perhaps 1 to 3 percent for interest-rate risk.[8] Suppose K is taken as the number of factors for which at least two β_{kit} are nonzero across the N assets; then realizations of these factors affect returns, but these factors are not necessarily priced in the sense of having nonzero factor risk premia (λ_{kt}s). In thick, liquid, integrated markets where arbitrage eliminates risk-free excess returns, the number of *priced* risk factors is likely much smaller than the total number of risk factors;[9] thus, ordering factors so that the first K' are priced, likely $K' \ll K$.

For the corporate decision maker assessing a project, the net present value approach is to discount expected cash flows at the appropriate risk-adjusted discount rate and undertake the project if net present value is greater than zero. In general, using a risk-adjusted discount rate larger (smaller) than appropriate leads to rejection of profitable projects (acceptance of unprofitable projects). In an economy described by (1) and (2), optimal capital allocation requires decision makers to use the expected rates of return ER_{it} in (2) as the discount rates in net present value decisions. Each project presents the decision maker with special problems in estimating expected cash flows and betas. Deciding on each project also requires knowledge of which risk factors are priced and of the sizes of the risk premia, but these priced factors and premia are the same for every project and decision maker; this opens the possibility of one decision maker using common knowledge, based on prior work of others, to simplify the decision process.[10]

The system (1)–(2) can be estimated with maximum likelihood methods. Substituting (2) into (1) gives

$$R_{it} = r_{ft} + \sum_{k=1}^{K'} \beta_{kit}\,\lambda_{kt} + \sum_{k=1}^{K} \beta_{kit}\,\delta_{kt} + e_{it}, \qquad i = 1,\ldots,N. \tag{3}$$

If the δ_{kt} are taken as observable, then the system (3) can be directly estimated. For example, for the U.S. Sweeney and Warga (1986a) use two factors, the rate of return on an equity market index and the surprise change in the yield on long-term government bonds.[11]

The number of factors K' must be estimated, as with all of the parameters in (3); this requires searching over various possible K' and using some reasonable criteria to decide on the optimal K'. Equation (3) shows parameters as time varying; for estimation purposes, it is often assumed that β_{kit}, λ_{kt}, σ_{eit} and $\sigma_{\delta kt}$ are time constant and that the risk factors (δs) are orthogonal to each other; for valid estimation, the e_{it} and the δ_{kt} must be orthogonal.[12]

Empirically, researchers find at least two priced factors. Roll and Ross (1981), using factor analysis, report that there are as many as five priced factors.[13] Chen, Roll and Ross (1986) report that changes in the log of industrial production, the change in expected inflation, the change in actual inflation and the differences in realized returns on different grades of bonds appear to be priced factors. Burmeister, Roll and Ross (1992) use a market factor and three bond-risk factors. Sweeney and Warga (1986a) report that when a market index is used as one factor, the change in the yield on long-term government bonds is priced. Using an approach similar to Sweeney and Warga's, Jorion (1991) finds little evidence that foreign exchange risk is priced. In general, it appears that when "the" market's rate of return is used as one factor, only a few other factors are priced.[14]

Integrated Capital Markets Reduce Information Requirements

Integration of capital markets allows the decision maker to free ride on any public information about the K' priced factors and the values λ_{kt}s of the risk premia; in this situation, the decision maker can devote resources to finding the project's β_{kit}s and expected cash flows.

The Arbitrage Pricing Theory gives no information on which factors are priced or the number of priced factors, that is, the K' factors with $\lambda_{kt} \neq 0$. In one interpretation, the Arbitrage Pricing Theory's main content is that the factor risk premia λ_{kt} are the same for all assets or projects i at time t; if two assets have nonzero β_{kt}s at t, then the expected rate of return of each increases by $\beta_{kit}\,\lambda_{kt}$ due to factor k. Similarly, if the K' priced factors are known for one asset in period t, the same K' are known for all assets. This Arbitrage Pricing Theory structure allows the decision maker to "piggyback" on the past work of others. For example, suppose that the priced factors are the same over time and that the risk premia λ_{kt} are time-constant;[15] then, from the work of others, the econometrician starts with informed rather than diffuse priors on K' and λ_{kt}, even if others have never examined the industry, firm or project that concerns the decision maker. To be sure, the decision maker must still estimate the relevant betas. The decision maker might estimate (3) as a single equation for asset i, with the β_{kit} estimated but the λ_{kt} constrained to equal the values others have estimated. The decision maker might use new data, in addition to those used to estimate K' and the λ_{kt}, to obtain updated, better estimates of the K' and the λ_{kt}. One relevant case is where an ongoing firm wants to estimate its equity cost of capital to be used for new projects believed to have the same risk characteristics as the firm; the firm can then estimate the β_{kit}s in (3) using time series of its own returns and the risk-free rate, with the λ_{kt}s taken as given.

The decision maker can piggyback in another way. The results on other, analogous work can be used to form priors on the β_{kit}s before estimation, or in the case where estimation is not possible (for example, a contemplated project with no data) to infer the β_{kit}s. Textbook advice (Brealey and Myers 1991) for finding betas for new projects is to start with the betas of firms with similar risk characteristics; a newly privatized steel company might look at betas of ongoing steel companies with shares traded on world markets.

Compare the above to a country that has substantially liberalized its trade accounts but allows no capital movements.[16] Except in extraordinary conditions, the country's capital markets are less than fully integrated with the world's. The appropriate risk-adjusted discount rates inside the country are very likely different from the outside world's. The set of priced factors in the country is likely to be $[K''] \neq [K']$; intuitively, the number of priced factors in this country is likely larger, $K'' > K'$, with K'' perhaps much larger than

K'. The set of factors $[K']$ need not be a subset of $[K'']$; indeed, the two sets need not intersect. The country's decision makers must identify these K'' factors as well as estimate the factor risk premia of the K'' factors and their projects' betas on these factors.[17]

With closed capital accounts, decision makers have to infer appropriate discount rates from domestic financial markets. These markets will be less informative than world markets,[18] and hence inference will be more difficult; the idiosyncratic terms e_{it} will have larger variances and hence the coefficients will have larger standard errors. Domestic decision makers cannot easily and directly piggyback on the research and skill of world-market investors; priors about risk factors—which are priced, their premia, projects' sensitivities to them—are more diffuse than under integration.[19]

With binding capital controls the country's domestic capital is misallocated. Investors get noisier, less informative capital-market signals about where to put funds across the domestic economy than they would from the world market under free capital mobility; too much capital goes in some areas, too little into others.

In the absence of capital controls, wealth holders in liberalizing countries choose portfolios governed by international risk considerations; capital controls restrict these wealth holders to suboptimal portfolios containing risk diversifiable in international markets. Thus, some important domestic investment decisions are likely governed by domestic risk considerations that are irrelevant internationally. That the country's capital markets likely do not allow as much scope for diversification as under integration with world markets is well understood; in fact, a frequent argument is that allowing capital outflows would likely result in substantial outflows as home-country residents rebalance their portfolios to gain from international diversification. There is no *a priori* reason to believe that these outflows would not be balanced by inflows as outside-world residents rebalance their portfolios.[20]

Capital Market Signals with Partial Financial Barriers

Few countries are totally cut off from world financial markets.[21] Partial capital account restrictions can, however, have major effects on the informativeness of capital-market signals. These effects depend on who is the marginal investor;[22] three cases are usefully distinguished. First, domestic residents subject to binding capital controls make the marginal investments; domestic decision makers face all of the problems discussed above in finding priced risk factors and estimating their premia; almost surely, signals about capital allocation are inferior to those obtainable with open capital accounts. Second, the government credibly commits to free repatriation and foreign investors make the marginal investment decisions. Third, the government does not credibly commit to free repatriation, but foreign investors nevertheless dominate investment decisions. These latter two cases, where foreign investors make the marginal decisions, add complications to the analysis, complications now discussed.

Foreign Capital Flows Unrestricted, Credible Repatriation Commitment, Domestic Outflows Restricted

Some observers urge liberalizing countries to restrict domestic outflows, but to allow free flows of foreign funds in and out, with the government credibly committed to repatriation. In this view, the country has too little foreign investment, so foreign investment is encouraged by allowing unrestricted foreign capital movements; because domestic capital flight is a significant possibility in this view, domestic outflows are restricted.

On the one hand, unrestricted foreign in- and outflows allow foreign investors to put funds in projects that offer expected rates of return that are adequate (or better) in terms of discount rates built on risk factors priced in world markets. If the government's commitment to free capital flows for foreigners is credible, then foreign investors dominate the liberalizing country's investment decisions, resulting in the same basket of projects as under free capital mobility for all. On the other hand, the domestic residents' portfolio is not diversified in world markets and hence contains risks that international markets ignore but which residents cannot ignore. Their portfolios consist in part of projects selected by foreign decision makers who ignore all but world-wide risks; these projects enter domestic portfolios through being joint ventures or ones where domestic firms hold majority or minority equity positions, or by being employers of domestic labor.[23] Capital market liberalization for foreigners but not for residents may result in more investment than otherwise, and will result in better capital allocation from a global viewpoint; the resulting domestic portfolio is suboptimal relative to what residents would hold if unrestricted. This suboptimality when residents' outflows are restricted might be used to argue for detailed government intervention in the choice of projects financed by foreigners. Given the great difficulties a government faces in knowing what is optimal for individual projects,[24] optimal policy may be to allow unrestricted capital mobility for both residents and foreigners. Of course, some observers might dismiss this conflict between actual and desired domestic portfolios as quantitatively unimportant in absolute terms or at least relative to claimed benefits.

Lack of Credible Commitment to Foreigners, Domestic Outflows Restricted

If the government's commitment to free capital flows for foreigners is not credible, foreigners use discount rates based on world-market risk factors, but apply these discount rates to lower expected values of cash flows to take account of the possibility of capital controls. Thus, foreign investment is lower than with credible commitment, and because foreign decision making is assumed to dominate in this case, the country's capital stock is lower. Residents hold a portfolio that does not take account of the risks they face, but only of world-market risk factors. Thus, lack of credible commitment likely results in a smaller level of capital in the economy than under credible commitment,[25] and leaves domestic wealth-holders with a more poorly diversified portfolio than under credible commitment to no capital controls.

More on Credibility

Countries that liberalize their capital accounts often are disappointed in the small inflow of foreign capital when this is allowed, and also worry about capital flight if capital outflows are allowed. One reason for disappointingly small capital inflows after liberalization is that promises that foreign investors may repatriate profits and capital lack credibility. In practice, repatriation requires or may require administrative clearance; for example, in many liberalizing countries, the international investor wishing to withdraw capital must satisfy the government that all tax obligations have been met. These administrative issues are subject to abuse to satisfy balance-of-payments or exchange-rate goals. Further, it is unclear when and how these restrictions may change. This is not to argue that the government is lying or intends to impose limits on foreign capital outflows. Instead, the issue is the credibility of the government's commitment to allow foreigners to move capital in the face of possible economic or political crises.[26,27]

Government restrictions on domestic residents' capital movements undermine credibility of promises that foreign investors can repatriate profits and capital. A liberalizing country with these restrictions says in effect that for now and in the future the optimum level of capital controls is not zero. Though the government's actions reveal that it currently thinks optimal controls are only on domestic residents, the foreign investor knows that in the future the government might decide the optimal level includes some transactions of foreign investors. The investor sees that the government is not committed to the principle of no restrictions as an intertemporally optimal policy, but rather believes that the optimal degree is variable. Further, the investor knows that the government realizes that its restrictions on domestic residents induce lower capital inflows than otherwise; the government's restrictions demonstrate its willingness to deter future capital inflows. This tells the foreign investor that funds are repatriatable just so long as the government thinks it politically profitable.

A government might instead adopt a policy of free capital movements for all. This increases the credibility of government promises of free capital movement for foreign funds. It exposes the government to larger capital outflows if people decide that government policy is on the wrong track; if the government adopts policies that appear economically detrimental, market reactions have even stronger exchange rate effects. Full convertibility signals that the government is confidant that it can and will pursue policies the market approves. Less-than-full convertibility announces that the government fears market reactions to its current and future policies; it raises wealth-holders' fears that future policies will deteriorate, and that this deterioration may include restrictions on foreigners' capital outflows.

A second reason that government promises of free repatriation are not fully credible is that much Western discussion suggests that capital controls are a useful or even necessary part of liberalizing countries' government policies. For example, some observers argue that after the Second World War, Western European countries took many years before allowing free capital mobility; the data argue that yields on short-term government securities on a covered basis reached equality only around 1985. In the European Community, Italy removed capital controls only in 1991, and Greece and Portugal had until 1995 to do the same;[28] if rich Western European countries took so long to remove capital controls, surely poorer liberalizing countries will have to take even longer. This argument implicitly assumes that Western European capital market restrictions were optimal. It might be argued that Western European restrictions were suboptimal and hindered recovery; if liberalizing countries follow the postwar policies of Western Europe, they too will take a very long time to recover. In another example, some observers argue that a payments union, perhaps along the lines of the postwar European Payments Union, might be useful for Eastern Europe. A similar payments union would institutionalize capital controls, signaling foreign investors that liberalizing-country governments view capital controls as a legitimate and useful policy tool.[29]

Conclusions

Many countries liberalize when their poor economic performance shows that restrictions on free markets can carry very heavy prices. Some of the liberalizing nations, and many of the economists offering advice, have learned this lesson better about goods markets than capital markets. Policy prescriptions often call for progressive goods market liberalization, starting right away. Discussions give serious consideration to the costs of delay in liberalizing goods markets, and demand substantial and substantiated benefits from proposed delays. Often delay in liberalizing capital accounts is taken for granted, with capital account liberalization to be undertaken only after substantial, successful goods market liberalization; this assumes low costs and possibly high benefits to delaying capital market liberalization.

A good investment is one where the expected rate of return is greater than the rate of return required on risk grounds. Financial markets provide information needed for appropriate intertemporal resource allocation, by allowing the observer to infer which risk factors are priced and the size of the risk premia for these factors. We have shown that if a liberalizing country's financial markets are integrated with world markets, the country benefits informationally in two ways. First, investment decisions in the liberalizing country are taken in terms of the risks important in the global context, not just in the country's context. Thus, decision makers do not have to start from scratch to find the risks important for the country. Second, it is easier to estimate risks internationally than for a particular isolated country; isolated markets provide information, but with more noise than international markets.

Many liberalizing countries promise foreigners free repatriation of capital and profits. The previous section discusses the way that restrictions on domestic capital outflows undermine the credibility of these promises. As a result, liberalizing countries likely receive less foreign investment than otherwise; their residents hold suboptimal portfolios; and the degree of capital misallocation is larger.

Liberalizing countries can build economic and financial institutions from scratch or import, or piggyback on, industrialized countries' institutions. It appears cheaper and more efficient to piggyback on well-developed foreign capital markets. Such piggybacking is an externality that benefits the liberalizing countries without harming (in fact, likely helping in a small way) the developed countries as a whole.[30]

Notes

This paper is part of the project on *Economic Security in an Unstable World;* parts of it were presented at a session of the Western Economics Association meetings, the Georgetown University Workshop on Financial Liberalization in Transitioning Economies, and the Estonia Conference on Financial Liberalization. Thanks for helpful discussions are due especially to Christine Ries, and to Thomas Brewer, Wlodek Burstyn, Vihang Errunza, Mark Taylor, Clas Wihlborg and Thomas Willett. Part of this paper was written at the Gothenburg (Sweden) School of Economics; summer grants from the Georgetown School of Business supported work on this paper, and the Georgetown University Center for Business-Government Relations provided partial summer research assistance.

1. Strategies to liberalize capital accounts differ widely. For example, by 1990 Poland had internal convertibility for residents and promises of free repatriation of profits and capital for foreign investors, greater liberalization than most Western European countries one decade after World War II and than many two decades after; contrarily, Russia has stringent capital controls, though capital outflows often evade the controls. In the latest round of liberalization, most Latin American countries have extensively liberalized goods markets before liberalizing policies on capital *in*flows, and wait even longer before liberalizing restrictions on capital *out*flows.

2. Hanson (1992) refers to this as the "traditional" argument for easing capital controls, as opposed to the later "diversification" argument that the country's citizens gain from access to foreign assets that allow them to diversify away non-systematic risk.

3. It is often argued that in this case foreigners "buy up" the country, meaning either that foreigners gain too much control of the country's resources or do not pay a high enough, fair price for the resources.

4. To be sure, observers sometimes raise problems of possible capital mis-allocation; see, for example, Crockett (1991), cited in Mathieson and Rojas-Suárez (1992). The usual strong focus on aggregate investment slights these micro allocation problems. Some observers point out that free markets are likely to do a better job of allocating capital than government direction; this is an argument for liberalizing domestic financial markets, however, not an argument for opening domestic financial markets to international competition.

5. The following discussion often focuses on equity markets for convenience, but bond markets are subject to the same points, *mutatis mutandis*.

6. More generally, r_{ft} may be replaced by E_{0t}, the expected rate of return on a portfolio with zero betas on all K risk factors.

7. The pricing relationship follows from the generating function under the assumption of no arbitrage profits in an infinite-asset economy (Ross 1976). Discrepancies between the text's pricing relationship and that in a finite-asset economy are argued to be quite small in an economy with a range of assets like the U.S.'s; see Dybvig (1986).

8. See Ibbotson (1990) for estimates of the risk premium on the market of perhaps 8 percent per annum. Sweeney and Warga (1986a) present estimates of the interest-rate risk premium of from perhaps 1 to 3 percent.

9. If the R_{it} are distributed such that they can be summarized by a mean vector and a covariance matrix, or if investors' utility functions are quadratic, then the only priced factor is "the" market, as in the Capital Asset Pricing Model.

10. Normative theory says that decision makers "should" use discount rates that take proper account of the priced risk factors. Positive theory says decision makers will approximately use such discount rates, even if the decision makers do not fully understand the Arbitrage Pricing Theory and its implications, and cannot verbalize the estimation necessary for computing the system parameters; the quality of the approximation depends, however, on the noise-signal ratio in financial markets.

11. If the δ_{kt} are taken as unobservable, maximum likelihood methods require simultaneous estimating of the δ_{kt} with (3). There is a large and complex literature on how to extract time series of realizations of unobserved factors (δs) and measure their

premia (λs); see Conway and Reinganum (1988). Sweeney and Warga (1986a, 1986b) discuss how even with observable risk factors, there is an identification problem in distinguishing λ_i from the sample mean δ_i.

12. Time variation in the σ_{eit} can be handled in principle by usual methods for correcting for heteroscedasticity. Time variations in the $\sigma_{\delta it}$ or correlation of the δ_{kt} require no change in methods. Correlation of the e_{it} and the δ_{kt} mean that the equations in (3) are not valid regression equations; the correlation must be modeled and can then be handled with standard methods. Similarly, time variation in λ_{kt} and β_{kit} must be modeled, for example, as first-order autoregressions, and can then be handled by standard methods.

13. Conway and Reinganum (1988) argue that conventional statistical approaches overstate the number of price factors and that there may well be only two priced factors.

14. If the rate of return on the market index used has no idiosyncratic risk, this market rate may be freely substituted for any priced factor; because the U.S. or world market portfolios are well diversified, the substitution seems plausible. To the extent that this rate of return has less measurement error and less idiosyncratic error than macro variables such as inflation or growth, the market factor may be expected to be the most important factor, a common result in the empirical literature.

15. This assumption is only for convenience. Even if the set of priced factors changes over time and the risk premia are also time varying, under very general conditions the econometrician benefits from the past work of others.

16. In the extensive literature on factor price equalization, unhindered mobility of goods is a perfect substitute for factor mobility under certain conditions. From observed differences in factor productivity and rewards across countries, liberalizing the trade account is not in fact a substitute for liberalizing the capital account.

17. Some observers believe this emphasis on risk-adjusted discount rates is misplaced.

Are all market betas unity? Empirically, many estimates of firms' market betas are within one or two standard errors of unity. On the other hand, market beta estimates for many firms are significantly different from unity. Further, beta estimates for industry portfolios have smaller standard errors than for firms, with the industry betas sometimes significantly different from unity. This implies that some if not all of the firms in such an industry have betas that are significantly different from unity.

Beta estimates show regression to the mean. For example, Blume (1975) shows that the betas farthest from unity in one time period show a strong tendency on average to be closer to unity in later estimation periods. Sharpe and Cooper (1972), however, show that there is substantial intertemporal stability of the deciles into which estimated betas fall; knowledge of a beta's decile in one period gives important information on its likely decile in the next.

An observer's unconditional prior about a firm's beta is unity. Priors conditioned on many cheap or free information sets are importantly different from unity, however. If the firm is an electric utility, the prior is that the firm's market beta is importantly less than unity.

Acceptable projects do not depend on the discount rate used. Some observers argue that, of projects firms accept, all or most have such high internal rates of return (IRRs) that any reasonable discount rate used is less than the internal rate of return. This view has some troubling implications, as the following example reveals. Suppose that the real risk-free rate is 1.0 percent/year; the risk premium on the market is 7.5 percent/year; the range of possible βs is $0.0 \leq \beta \leq 2.0$, so the range of required rates of return is 1.0 percent/year $\leq ER \leq$ 16 percent/year; the initial investment, I, is \$1. In this case, for a project to be acceptable without regard to the discount rate used, the present value of the expected cash flows (ECF) must exceed \$1 for all possible required rates of return. Assuming the expected cash flows are a perpetuity, then $ECF/.16 \geq \$1$. Similarly, for a project to be unattractive no matter how low the discount rate, $ECF/.01 \leq \$1$. Thus, when cash flows are converted to (perpetual) annuity equivalents, the vast majority of projects must have $ECF/I \geq .16$ or $ECF/I \leq .01$; loosely, projects either have internal rates of return greater than 16 percent or internal rates of return that are negative or only trivially positive. Similarly, most projects then have payback periods of either under seven years or more than a hundred years. Further, if project decisions were usually so clear cut, there would not be such intra-firm conflicts over what divisional hurdle rates to use.

Is the premium on the market approximately zero? For the postwar period, the average rate of return on the market has not been significantly greater than the average risk-free rate, or the risk premium on the market has not been significantly positive. Sweeney and Warga (1986b) point out that the estimate of the market premium in traditional security market line tests (Fama and McBeth 1973; Black, Jensen and Scholes 1972) is really an estimate of the sample risk premium over the period considered. Recent work by Fama and French (1992) finds that the estimated market premium in security market line tests is insignificant; this is not surprising given the postwar data.

This might suggest that difficulties in estimating betas and the market risk premium are irrelevant; if the risk premium is essentially zero, there is no need to estimate it and betas.

Much work, however, finds important priced risk factors even if the market is neglected. In general, using models more complex than a simple market model to handle risk increases the informational difficulties for liberalizing countries. Predetermined explanatory variables that use accounting numbers, for example, earnings-price and book-to-market ratios, are difficult to construct in economies where few firms are publicly traded, generally accepted accounting practices differ from industrialized countries, and the meaning and accuracy of accounting numbers are more obscure than usual.

18. Stock markets in Eastern Europe and the former Soviet Union may be among the less informative of the "emerging markets." In some cases, there are few stocks traded (for example, only a little over twenty-five on the Warsaw exchange), meaning it is difficult to infer movements in the "true" market that is composed of many more assets. Further, the market may be thin and illiquid (for example, more than 1,000 stocks listed in the Czech Republic as a result of the privatization process). Trades can be infrequent, and transactions of relatively modest dollar value can cause substantial price moves. Some observers believe such markets are more subject to manipulation or to endogenous bubbles than are, say, the U.S. and U.K. markets.

Because of thin and infrequent trading, some observers argue that daily prices are not useful time series for estimating asset pricing models; under the rule of thumb that sixty time-series observations are needed for estimating asset pricing models on monthly data, for many stocks there will be insufficient data until the late 1990s. Even then these markets' data are problematic: Many emerging-market stocks show evidence of thin and infrequent trading even in monthly data; domestic market indices often are dominated by one or a few stocks.

19. With the trade accounts closed, world goods prices are not optimal signals for internal resource allocation; producing at world prices gives suboptimal allocation unless goods can be traded internationally at those prices. Similarly, using discount rates derived from world markets is optimal only if owners of the country's capital can form portfolios over the international market.

20. A small, specialized country may well find that the percentage of wealth its residents want to devote to rebalancing is larger than for a large country with much domestic diversification. Because the outside world has so much more total wealth, only a modest rebalancing of the outside world's portfolio is needed to offset the liberalizing country's outflows.

21. An extensive literature on cross-country financial market integration assumes that residents of countries with capital controls on in- and outflows can in fact hold foreign securities in desired proportions but that residents of countries without controls cannot hold securities of countries that have controls. If investors care only about the first and second moments of distributions of current returns, investors resident in countries with restrictions hold the world market portfolio and only world market risk is priced, while residents in countries without restrictions hold less diversified portfolios and for them risk factors other than the world market might be priced. See Errunza *et al.* (1992) for discussion and tests. Models of this type assume that costs of evading capital controls are negligible (at least not prohibitive) for residents of countries with restrictions and that these are "large" countries in the sense that their assets comprise a fraction of world assets that cannot be ignored for analyzing the pricing of risk. I assume that countries with restrictions are "small" in the sense that they have no effect on parameters in the risk model in (1) and (2).

22. This discussion contrasts foreign and domestic investors. It could be phrased in terms of investors facing both domestic and rest-of-the-world opportunities, versus investors facing only domestic opportunities. This formulation would allow for the possibility that some domestic residents, owing to porous controls on domestic outflows, are able to act as if unconstrained by controls (Errunza *et al.* 1992). Presumably these investors are for the most part rich, though increasing porousness over time makes these opportunities increasingly available to the less rich.

23. The investor's optimal portfolio accounts for risk/return contributions of financial assets but also the investor's human capital (Amacher and Sweeney 1981).

24. The domestic equities market may or may not be dominated by foreigners and hence international considerations. If foreigners dominate the equities market, then it will be impossible to extract from the market the risk factors important to domestic residents. If foreigners do not dominate the markets, the risk factors can be extracted, but the estimates of which factors are priced and their premia are noisier

than under integration both for the reasons discussed in the text and because the market gives only partial weight to the domestic risks that foreigners ignore.

25. This depends on whether wealth or substitution effects dominate. Because the marginal unit of wealth has a smaller risk-adjusted expected return than under integrated markets, the average domestic saver may hold a smaller stock of wealth; or, he may focus on the higher risks he faces and decide to hold a larger stock of wealth.

26. Industrial countries often impose selective controls during political crises. For example, the U.S. froze Iranian assets during the 1979–81 hostage crisis and froze Iraqi and (for a time) Kuwaiti assets after Iraq's August 1990 invasion of Kuwait. In many countries, economic crises quickly become political crises.

27. There are two ways that the possibility of exchange restrictions reduces the expected net present value of an investment. First, it reduces the expected cash flow from an investment. For example, with a bond the best that can happen is that the investor gets the promised cash flows and is allowed to convert them into foreign currency; possible exchange controls reduce the expected value of these promises without any offsetting upside risk. Second, if the imposition of exchange controls is correlated with any priced risk factor in the international economy, the possibility of exchange controls raises the project's beta on that risk factor and hence the risk-adjusted discount rate used to evaluate the expected cash flows.

28. In the aftermath of the European Community currency crisis of September 1992, Ireland, Portugal and Spain put on some capital controls. In May/June 1994, Greece relaxed capital controls, causing a huge outflow of capital and a currency crisis for the drachma.

29. If a government embraces a payments union rather than credibly committing to free capital flows, this is likely to cause substantially reduced capital inflows. The observed effect of a payments union may be quite small, however, because investors who doubt a government's commitment to free capital flows will put relatively little at risk. With a payments union in place, strengthening or loosening it may have little absolute effect on the small amount of foreign investment.

30. If there are no real externalities in market formation, the effects on developed economies are simply a pecuniary externality. In this case, the western market participants who benefit can compensate westerners who lose and still be better off on net; this is a terms-of-trade improvement for the West as a whole relative to the liberalizing countries. It may be that there are congestion externalities in market making, so that Western market makers are better off but Western economies as a whole are worse off. On balance, it seems more likely that there are economies of scale in markets so that the West will be better off as a whole.

References

Amacher, Ryan, and Richard J. Sweeney. 1981. "On the Integration of United States Labor Markets: A Definition and Test of the Radical Segmentation Hypothesis." *Journal of Labor Research* 2(1): 25–37.

Black, Fisher, Michael C. Jensen, and Myron Scholes. 1972. "The Capital Asset Pricing Model: Some Empirical Tests," in Michael C. Jensen, ed., *Studies in the Theory of Capital Markets*. New York: Praeger.

Blume, Marshall. 1975. "Betas and their Regression Tendencies." *Journal of Finance* 30(3): 785–95.

Brealey, Richard, and Stewart Myers. 1991. *Principles of Corporate Finance*, 4th ed. New York: McGraw-Hill.

Burmeister, Edwin, Richard Roll, and Stephen A. Ross. 1992. "A Practitioner's Guide to Arbitrage Pricing Theory." Duke University Working Paper.

Chen, Nai-fu, Richard Roll, and Stephen A. Ross. 1986. "Economic Forces and the Stock Market." *Journal of Business* 59(3): 383–403.

Conway, Delores A., and Marc R. Reinganum. 1988. "Stable Factors in Security Returns: Identification Using Cross-Validation." *Journal of Business and Economic Statistics* 6(1): 1–15.

Crockett, Andrew. 1991. "Financial Market Implications of Trade and Currency Zones." International Monetary Fund Working Paper, Washington, D.C.

Dybvig, Philip. 1986. "An Explicit Bound on Deviations from APT Pricing in a Finite Economy." *Journal of Financial Economics* 12(4): 483–96.

Errunza, Vihang, Etienne Losq and Prasad Padmanabhan. 1992. "Test of Integration, Mild Segmentation and Segmentation Hypotheses." *Journal of Banking and Finance* 16(5): 949–72.

Fama, Eugene, and Kenneth R. French. 1992. "The Cross-Section of Expected Stock Returns." *Journal of Finance* 47(2): 427–65.

Fama, Eugene, and James D. McBeth. 1973. "Risk, Return and Equilibrium: Empirical Tests." *Journal of Political Economy* 81(3): 607–36.

Hanson, James. 1992. "Opening the Capital Account: A Survey of Issues and Results." *Policy Research Working Papers*, WPS 901. Washington, D.C.: World Bank.

Ibbotson Associates. 1990. *Stocks, Bonds, Bills and Inflation: 1990 Yearbook.* Chicago.

Jorion, Philippe. 1991. "The Pricing of Exchange Rate Risk in the Stock Market." *Journal of Financial and Quantitative Analysis* 26(3): 363–76.

Mathieson, Donald J., and Liliana Rojas-Suárez. 1992."Liberalization of the Capital Account: Experiences and Issues." *IMF Working Paper* No. 92/46. Washington, D.C.: International Monetary Fund.

McKinnon, Ronald I. 1991. *The Order of Economic Liberalization.* Baltimore: Johns Hopkins University Press.

Roll, Richard, and Stephen A. Ross. 1981. "An Empirical Investigation of the Arbitrage Pricing Theory." *Journal of Finance* 35(5): 1073–103.

Ross, Stephen A. 1976. "The Arbitrage Theory of Capital Asset Pricing." *Journal of Economic Theory* 13(3): 341–60.

Sharpe, William F., and Guy Cooper. 1972. "Risk-Return Classes of NYSE Stocks, 1931–67." *Financial Analysts Journal* 28 (March/April).

Sweeney, Richard J., and Arthur D. Warga. 1986a. "The Pricing of Interest-Rate Risk: Evidence from the Stock Market." *Journal of Finance* 41(2): 393–410.

———. 1986b. "The Possibility of Estimating Risk Premia." *The Financial Review* 21(2): 163–82.

Williamson, John. 1996. "Orthodoxy Is Right: Liberalize the Capital Account Last." Chapter 2 in this volume.

5

Currency Convertibility, Policy Credibility and Capital Flight in Poland and the Czech and Slovak Federal Republic

David G. Dickinson and Andrew W. Mullineux

Introduction

This chapter considers some aspects of exchange rate policy for formerly centrally planned economies during their transition to "market economies." In particular, the relationship between (currency) convertibility, capital outflows (flight) and policy credibility is examined. These factors are mutually related, and their interaction is highlighted by focusing on the experiences of Poland and the (ex) Czech and Slovak Federal Republic.[1] These countries are in the vanguard of emerging market economies and their experience provides a basis for policy recommendations for emerging market economies at an earlier stage in their transitions. The analysis also allows for discussion of the speed at which the emerging market economies could move to a fully convertible currency.

Three distinct (but related) areas of analysis, each of which has been the subject of a large amount of research, are synthesized. The issue of convertibility in the case of transforming former socialist economies has been analyzed in considerable detail (Williamson 1991; Greene and Isard 1991) and will be considered in the next section. The problem of capital outflows from countries which need to retain as much internal finance for investment as possible has also generated considerable interest.[2] Of particular relevance is the work on capital outflows from developing, particularly Latin American, economies (Lessard and Williamson 1987). The measurement and explanation of capital flight will be considered in the third section. Since risks are cited as a major reason for capital flight, the issue of policy credibility also rests neatly within the analysis of capital flight. However, we need to be more specific about what factors lend a policy stance credibility, particularly for economies which are undergoing major structural adjustment. This issue is examined in the fourth section, where the discussion of policy credibility is related back to the issue of capital flight. Following this, the analysis of the earlier sections is used to examine the specific cases of Poland and the (ex) Czech and Slovak Republic. The macroeconomic experiences of these two countries differ quite considerably, and it will be of interest to examine how the diverse performance of the two economies impacted upon the degree of capital flight. This will provide insight into the causes of such outflows. The final section draws together the main elements of the analysis and suggests some criteria which can be employed to determine the timing of a move to full convertibility. It also discusses the appropriate exchange rate policy for emerging market economies at an earlier stage in their transition.

Foreign Exchange Convertibility

Foreign exchange convertibility may be limited to current account transactions or extended through a spectrum of interim stages to full, current and capital account, convertibility. The terms internal and external convertibility are also frequently used. There are slight differences in the meaning of each of these terms, as we now explain.[3]

Current account convertibility relates to individuals' rights to obtain foreign exchange at the prevailing market rate, in order to conduct normal international trade in goods in accordance with the IMF's Articles of Agreement. One way to achieve this is to permit internal convertibility, whereby domestic residents have the right to hold domestic deposits of foreign currency. Internal convertibility gives incentives for domestic residents to operate through the official markets and to move away from black market operations, which were an endemic feature of the former centrally planned economies. Current account transactions can, however, be restricted under internal convertibility—by the imposition of tariffs and quotas for example—and internal convertibility can be curtailed under current account convertibility. In many countries foreign exchange controls prohibit the holding of foreign exchange accounts at banks but allow the purchase of limited amounts of foreign exchange for business and holiday trips abroad. Furthermore, the establishment of internal convertibility makes the control of capital outflows harder to detect. Capital flight can become a real policy problem if capital outflows cannot be controlled, and "dollarization," which can be regarded as repressed capital flight, may result if they can.

Capital account or external convertibility is achieved by the extension of access to foreign exchange for the conduct of cross-border trade in both financial and real assets through the removal of all foreign exchange controls. The integration of the financial sector into the international community can have major benefits for the efficient allocation of capital and allows domestic enterprises full access to international sources of finance. The possibility of substantial capital outflows as a result of the high risks associated with domestic currency assets while the credibility of the economic transformation program is being established, means that it is not possible to establish this level of convertibility at an early stage in the transformation process. However, repatriation of profits is a necessary precondition for foreign direct investment to be forthcoming, and the ability to repatriate investment capital is also desirable. For this reason emerging market economies, which need to generate capital inflows to supplement low domestic savings pools, typically combine restricted (especially for the non-trading sector) internal and current account convertibility with capital account convertibility for foreign investors while maintaining restrictions on domestic capital outflows.

Problems relating to currency convertibility, and exchange rate policy in general, have been recognized as key issues needing to be tackled by the transforming economies of Central and Eastern Europe. The basic argument for current account convertibility is that it exposes domestic producers to the full rigor of international competition and ensures that the pricing of key inputs, particularly energy, is consistent with world market conditions, thereby revealing comparative advantages and disadvantages and enhancing microeconomic efficiency.[4] The monopoly power of state-owned firms is consequently countervailed in the run-up to commercialization and privatization, and behavioral changes are imposed on enterprise managers. The adoption of current account convertibility, along with trade liberalization and the removal of distortionary price subsidies, was regarded as an important step in the process of promoting a market economy, and was adopted at the outset of the transitions in Poland (in January 1990) and the Czech and Slovak Republic (in January 1991). To achieve current account convertibility, it is necessary to unify the official and black-market exchange rates. This normally entails devaluing the "official" rate substantially. The choice of the appropriate initial exchange rate, especially if a fixed, rather than a floating, exchange rate regime is to be adopted is, however, a bit of a "stab in the dark." This is because the parallel market rate is likely to be lower than the free market rate due to the restricted nature of the parallel market and its varying level of liquidity.

If a fixed exchange target is to be pursued, it is necessary to allow for the upward price adjustment necessary to eliminate shortages resulting from the removal of subsidies and the introduction of a value-added or a similar consumption tax. Poland and the Czech and Slovak Republic both chose initial exchange rates close to the prevailing black market rates and thus over- devalued, or undervalued, their currencies by choice. The problem of choosing the initial rate of exchange implies that a crawling peg, and possibly real exchange rate targeting, may be a more appropriate, and therefore a more credible, option than nominal exchange rate targeting. In the absence of adequate foreign exchange reserves, and hence in effect support from overseas for a fixed exchange rate policy, a floating exchange rate becomes the only credible option. The adoption of real exchange rate targeting is of dubious validity given the problem of identifying an equilibrium real rate. This problem is compounded in transition economies which are undergoing massive restructuring. Another reason for adopting fixed exchange rates is that they may restrain inflation by restraining wage increases in the traded goods sector. The restraint is only effective, however, if the currency is not undervalued. Under the floating and real exchange rate targeting options, convertibility does not result in the exchange rate serving as a nominal anchor and an alternative must be sought. Because they chose to undervalue their currencies, Poland and the Czech and Slovak Republic initially opted for tax-based income policies to control wage inflation. As a result of undervaluation, both countries developed balance of trade surpluses, but upward price level adjustment and persistent inflation soon began to appreciate the real exchange rate and the trade surpluses were eroded. The more rapid inflation in Poland led to the adoption of a crawling peg when the trade deficit emerged in May 1991. To contain the deficit, supplementary devaluations were required. In contrast, the Czech and Slovak Republic, and since January 1993, the Czech Republic, has maintained its fixed exchange rate and has continued to run a trade surplus throughout the transition. Its inflation rate remained above those of its trading partners, however, and consequently the real exchange rate continued to appreciate. If the inflation differential remains positive, the nominal exchange rate constraint will begin to bite and the exchange rate policy may have to be adjusted. The need to change the policy will depend on the credibility of the government's anti-inflation stance and, therefore, on the reputation it has managed to build. The extent to which its anti-inflationary reputation would be damaged by a move to a crawling peg regime was openly debated among policymakers in the country.

Full (current and capital account) currency convertibility is a recent postwar phenomena among major OECD countries and followed the progressive removal of exchange controls in the 1980s (Mathieson and Rojas-Suárez 1993). It should be recognized, however, that the credibility of the reform process can be enhanced by a well-timed move to full convertibility at an appropriate exchange rate with a coherent exchange rate policy and adequate foreign exchange reserves. There is a balance to be struck between the credibility enhancement of a fully convertible currency and the risk of large-scale capital outflows in response to the high risks associated with domestic financial assets. In discussing the impact of full capital account convertibility, the issue of capital flight naturally arises. It is to this subject that the analysis now turns.

Capital Flight and Its Causes

The problem of capital flight attracted considerable interest in the mid-1980s because of its alleged role in aggravating the Third-World debt problem. There is no generally accepted definition of the term, and even if a definition could be agreed upon, substantial measurement problems would remain. Williamson and Lessard (1987) review literature on the subject and argue that capital flight should not be viewed, narrowly, as the illegal export of capital resulting from attempts to circumvent foreign exchange controls.[5] It should instead include all outflows of capital that exceed "normal" levels. This makes it virtually impossible to quantify because the standard measurement problems are compounded by the need to identify "normal" capital outflows.[6] However, the concept of policy credibility could help pin down the meaning of "normal," in the sense that as long as policy is credible there will still be some capital outflow (and inflow) emanating from rational portfolio adjustment decisions of international investors. This approach would need to be tempered with recognition of the constraints on portfolio diversification, which is where the degree of convertibility is important.

Given the substantial measurement problems, this analysis focuses primarily on private capital outflows and no attempt is made to identify which part of these outflows is "normal" and which part can be regarded as "abnormal." For economies embarking on the transition to a market economy, the problem of identifying normal outflows is compounded by the likelihood that, following the introduction of convertibility, at least some portfolio diversification is be expected and some overshooting of asset positions could well take place. Note that a countervailing balance exists in terms of foreign direct investment. It should also be noted that a characteristic of these economies is that, prior to the reform process, significant holdings of foreign currencies (particularly the dollar) by domestic residents, for use on the black markets, were common.[7] As noted, these balances can be regarded as representing "repressed" capital flight. They are normally legalized as part of the restructuring process, a policy which is designed to "capture" them within the domestic financial system.[8] This may be particularly important when attempting to establish convertibility at a fixed exchange rate with limited foreign exchange reserves, as Poland and the Czech and Slovak Republic attempted to do. The presence of such holdings needs to be taken into account in any analysis of capital flight and will be discussed below.

Even if foreign exchange controls are impregnable, capital flight can, and does, occur through "misinvoicing."[9] This involves under-invoicing exports, so that some of the foreign exchange earned by exporters can be placed in overseas bank accounts, and over-invoicing imports, so that more foreign exchange can be obtained from the banks than strictly required. In the latter case, the "excess" foreign exchange has to be illegally removed from the country somehow. To the extent that these activities result in the growth of foreign exchange deposits held by transition countries' residents in overseas bank accounts and is the main cause of this deposit growth, figures on such deposits can be used to gauge the scale of the capital flight resulting from misinvoicing. Misinvoicing can be reduced by more effective policing by customs and excise authorities. To achieve this, international cooperation is clearly required and the level of policing necessary to reduce misinvoicing significantly would be costly. Note that firms may also under-invoice imports to escape restrictions on the value of goods bought overseas (Gulati 1987).

The formerly centrally planned economies, which embarked on the transformation process with extremely basic "two-tier" bank-based financial systems, are unable to offer as wide a range of financial assets as more developed countries.[10] Hence, due to portfolio diversification and risk management, a potentially large capital outflow is to be anticipated. This may be reversed as the financial sector develops, privatization progresses, and secondary equity and government bond markets are established. If we could ignore this important factor, we would expect outflows and inflows to be determined by relative real interest rates on bank accounts and yields on other securities (net of tax), adjusted for risks. It is this reasoning which has underpinned the theoretical and empirical analysis of capital flight (e.g. Cuddington 1986; Lessard and Williamson 1987; Rojas-Suárez 1991). Application of conventional asset management theory (Markowitz 1991) leads to standard models of portfolio selection in which a balance is struck between risk and return and the appropriate mix of different financial instruments is determined. In this context, capital flight would reflect the failure of domestic financial assets to provide a return which is commensurate with the perceived risks of holding that asset.

Two reasons have been advanced for the failure of returns on domestic assets to fully compensate for the differential risks. One is that the risks are so large that rates of return cannot provide sufficient compensation without the imposition of extremely high nominal interest rate levels and the consequent collapse in aggregate demand. The other explanation is that differential treatment of domestic and foreign investors (in favor of those from abroad) creates an incentive for "round-tripping," whereby capital flows illegally out of the country so that it can return (via external borrowing) and take advantage of the favorable conditions created to encourage inward investment (Khan and Ul Haque 1985). Such policy measures usually take the form of some guarantee to foreign investors, which will carry significant value in situations where there are high risks of repudiation of debt or penal taxation/expropriation of interest. Hence we are left to conclude that it is the perceived risks of investing domestically which are crucial to the analysis of capital flight, the key insight being that such perceptions are dependent on whether investment is from outside or within the domestic economy. This differential risk view implies that capital outflow will, to some extent, be matched by an inflow resulting from borrowing abroad by domestic residents.

In order to explain capital flight, the risks faced by investors in domestic assets must first be identified. Essentially there are two categories which need to be considered: risks due to shocks hitting the economy, and risks resulting from policy actions, perhaps in response to economic outcomes. In this latter category, fiscal and monetary policy actions should be distinguished, since this will assist in relating analysis of risks to the credibility of economic policy.

In the context of non-policy shocks, the transforming economies are subject to the vagaries of the world economic environment. In addition, the reform program itself creates a high level of uncertainty. Sources of economic shocks which increase uncertainty and which have made domestic financial assets particularly risky include the collapse of traditional (CMEA) export markets; the need for large-scale resource reallocation in response to a move to world price structures; the possibility of major bankruptcies, large output losses and an increase in unemployment; and the need to restructure the underdeveloped financial sector.

Such major changes in the domestic economic environment create the potential for unexpected policy developments. In the context of fiscal policy, transition economies face large-scale government funding difficulties. The "transition recession" creates a need to establish, virtually from scratch, a "social safety net" to make the reform politically acceptable. Massive outlays are also needed to facilitate enterprise, and particularly bank, restructuring in order to deal with the "debt overhang" prior to privatization (see Mullineux 1992a, 1992b, 1994). Meanwhile state enterprises, which provided the majority of "tax" revenue under central planning, can be expected to experience declining "profitability" during the transition. A new tax system has to be devised and introduced from scratch and may cause "inflationary blips" of uncertain magnitude.[11] As with other institutional changes, such as the introduction of bankruptcy laws needed to "harden budget constraints" and the introduction of laws delineating "restitution" and property rights which are a necessary prerequisite to launching privatization programs and before foreign direct investment can be attracted, this takes time. Hence, it may be difficult to fund the budget deficit other than by imposing an inflation tax through "borrowing" from the central bank. In addition, the state-owned enterprise debt problem can be regarded as an off-balance-sheet national liability or debt (Begg and Portes 1992). This problem needs to be resolved, as part of the bank and state-owned enterprise restructuring process, prior to privatization. If the government takes on the debt, then its debt servicing charges will increase and financial assistance from international institutions is clearly desirable.

The need to deal with the monetary overhang inherited from the planned system is the first major problem for monetary policy. The overhang creates a risk of high inflation given that the alternative solution, currency reform, is politically unpopular.[12] Developing a financial system able to meet the demands of a free-market economy is the next major step. As discussed above, the very rudimentary nature of the inherited financial system creates an incentive for portfolio investment abroad. The impact of monetary policy also becomes more difficult to predict in periods of (financial) institutional change. The creation of an independent central bank is one route towards clarity, but does not immediately boost credibility because the central bank needs to build a reputation. An alternative means of boosting credibility is to use the exchange rate as a nominal anchor. The latter policy choice, however, introduces additional uncertainty relating to future government commitment to the fixed exchange rate. Again, it will take time to build credibility. Clearly, the extent of foreign exchange risk depends, at least in the short run, on the level of the initial exchange rate in relation to the positive inflation differential with major trading partners. If, at the start of the reform process, a country has significantly undervalued its currency, then the risk of devaluation in the near future should be quite low. Alternatively it can be argued that overvaluation of the currency enhances the credibility of the anti-inflationary commitment by ensuring appropriately tough monetary and fiscal policies; but this does not appear to be a feasible option for countries experiencing extreme shocks to their underlying economic structure, possessing limited foreign exchange reserves, and needing to re-orientate trade.

The credibility of the reform package as a whole, and the macroeconomic stabilization program in particular, is a key factor in assessing the risks inherent in domestic financial assets relative to those abroad, and hence the risk premium required to ensure that only "normal" capital flows take place. In the next section factors which influence the credibility of policy are considered.

Policy Credibility and Capital Flight

For the emerging market economies, the problem of policy credibility is of a different order of magnitude to that usually discussed in the macroeconomics literature.[13] In these countries, the aim is to change the nature of resource allocation. To do this, initiatives are required at both the micro and macro levels, and the success of the program depends upon delivering the desired result at both levels. It is necessary for successful macro-stabilization to complement enterprise reform. Without a stable aggregate environment, enterprises cannot be expected to make efficient resource allocation decisions. Capital flight is clearly just one element in the adjustment process, but its analysis highlights how policy credibility is the key to a successful program. In addition, the level of capital flight may provide an indicator of the credibility of the reform program. If "credibility" can be measured in this way, then the relationship between policy decisions and credibility can be explored.[14]

The last section has indicated that there is a close relationship between risks of holding financial assets and policy credibility.[15] For example, the credibility of the attempt to control inflation can be taken as an indicator of devaluation risk, since if inflation is higher in the transition economies than in their major trading partners, real exchange rate appreciation occurs when there is a fixed rate currency peg. This increases the probability of devaluation, unless of course the currency was substantially undervalued in the first place and the inflation differential disappears before the undervaluation is eliminated.[16] In a similar way, the credibility of monetary restraint is damaged by fiscal deficits which seem out of control.

Institutional factors can also influence the credibility of policy. The government may lack the power to curb wage demands in the early stages of the reform, prior to widespread "commercialization" and privatization, when workers have a large degree of control over enterprise behavior (as in Poland). A major economic collapse creates political tensions which threatens instability and increases the "risk of policy reversal" (as in Russia). The relationship between cohesiveness of the political structure and the success and credibility of the reform process is extremely important.[17] Lack of political consensus will almost certainly generate capital flight, given the great uncertainties it engenders.[18] However, even if the majority support a redistribution of economic power to the detriment of the *nomenklatura* (see below), the latter will have an incentive to get the wealth they control out of the country.

Policy initiatives may be required because of unexpected economic developments which render the announced initiatives suboptimal. Thus revisions to the policy stance may not necessarily reflect a lack of commitment on the part of policymakers. There is a problem in determining the motives of governments, and hence the credibility of policy, when exogenous shocks cause optimal policy choices to change unexpectedly. Governments may renege on earlier commitments and blame uncontrollable economic events for this decision. For the honest government, there is a tradeoff which will exist between changing the policy and suffering some loss of credibility, and sticking to a policy which is no longer optimal. As noted above, this dilemma has already been faced in Poland, and may be faced in the next year or so in the Czech Republic with respect to exchange rate policy, specifically, the maintenance of a fixed exchange rate while the trade balance deteriorates.

Not only do risks emanate from policy changes in response to unexpected economic events but also from political developments. Political stability is an important deterrent to capital flight. If there is a democratic consensus favoring reform, then the credibility argument implies that a critical mass of reforms should be introduced at an early stage, in an attempt to render the process of transformation irreversible and hence politically untouchable. Such a change inevitably involves (at least potentially) transferring economic power (and redistributing income) from the elite under the centrally planned system (the *nomenklatura*) to other economic agents and newly created institutions. The *nomenklatura* is likely to resist change, unless it can benefit from it, and political opposition to the "marketization" of the economy is therefore likely. The *nomenklatura*, which included the wealthiest individuals under the old regime, would be expected, for example, to favor privatization by auctions, rather than via mass distribution of vouchers, and may generally oppose rapid reform and try to maintain the power of the military-industrial complex. Hence, there is a need for policy changes to be sufficiently bold to prevent a reversion to the old order. Further, if conditions have deteriorated substantially, such as in Poland following the 1989 hyperinflation, bold policy initiatives are more likely to attract widespread public support, which in turn enhances their credibility.[19] The current success of China, however, indicates that policy credibility can also be achieved through a consensus-building gradual reform process and that the transition recession can be avoided in the process; but note that this is within a very restrictive political regime. The failure of "gradualism" in Poland and Hungary in the 1980s suggests that the tendency to treat all emerging market economies in the same way is inadvisable and that each country should be tackled individually because of their different histories and their political inheritances. That having been said, there may be certain general conclusions that can be drawn about issues such as the appropriate exchange rate policy for emerging market economies.

There is disagreement over exactly what the "critical mass" or "minimum bang" reform package should include, but there is a fairly broad consensus (Williamson 1991) that it should include the "hardening of budget constraints" (Kornai 1990) or "stabilization," price liberalization, commodity convertibility,[20] import liberalization, and also current account or internal convertibility. Williamson (1991) argues that the Czech and Slovak Republic introduced something close to a "minimum bang" in January 1991, while Poland's January 1990 "big bang" went further in that the initial price liberalization and subsidy removal was more comprehensive and the stabilization program was, of necessity, more draconian. As indicated above, this may be a reflection of the less favorable starting point in the Polish case.

There is a close relationship between the decision to introduce convertibility and policy credibility. The case for the inclusion of current account convertibility in a "minimum bang" package at an early stage of the transition process is that it can potentially add credibility to the macro-stabilization (budget and monetary restraint) component of the program and facilitate a rapid restructuring process. Commodity convertibility and price liberalization are unlikely to be sufficient on their own to bring about a rapid adjustment of relative prices to those prevailing elsewhere in the world. Trade liberalization and current account convertibility are also required and will help to induce an efficient allocation of resources and an inflow of foreign investment. Credibility is, however, a two-way street. Currency convertibility itself cannot just be imposed by policymakers. It has to be "earned" or achieved by being combined with a credible package of policies, and there must be a credibly large foreign exchange reserve (perhaps with international assistance promised) as a back-up if a fixed or crawling peg, rather than a floating exchange rate policy, is to be adopted. The absence of a foreign currency (external) debt problem also adds to the credibility of a non-floating exchange rate policy. In Poland's case, the introduction of current account convertibility in January 1990 was soon followed by a credibility bolstering agreement with the major (official) international creditors to a sizeable, conditional (on performance), and staged, write-down of debt liabilities and the establishment of an IMF-sponsored stabilization fund to back the convertible zloty. As noted above, in response to significant real exchange rate appreciation, this policy gave way to a crawling peg during 1991. In the case of the Czech and Slovak Republic, the external debt problem was minor, and the country had traditionally pursued conservative fiscal policies and had hardly experimented with reforms at all, unlike the other Visegrad countries (Poland and Hungary).[21]

In sum, successful policy requires credibility. Capital flight responds to the relative risks of investing at home and abroad, and the degree of policy credibility is an important influence on risk assessment. The adoption of currency convertibility can add credibility to the overall policy stance, but the other components of policy must be consistent with convertibility for it to have the desired beneficial effects. The degree of convertibility permitted will be closely related to the degree of credibility of the overall policy stance. Even without full convertibility, the problem of capital flight means that governments should strive to make their chosen policy as credible as possible.[22] Otherwise, the costs of the reform process in terms of an even harsher macroeconomic stabilization package involving, for example, high nominal and real interest rates to support the exchange rate, will be greater.

In the next section, the determination of capital outflows from Poland and the Czech and Slovak Republic during the period since current account convertibility was established through the end of 1992 is investigated.

An Analysis of Capital Flight in Poland and the Czech and Slovak Federal Republic

The analysis of the evidence of capital flight, and possible reasons for its existence, relates to the early stage of the transition for both Poland (1990–92) and the Czech and Slovak Republic (1991–92). This can be characterized as the macro-stabilization phase, in which policymakers were required to adopt harsh monetary and fiscal policies in order to create a sound macroeconomic environment and enhance their credibility with international institutions such as the IMF and the World Bank. A considerable amount of analysis of this period has been conducted—see, e.g., Begg (1991) and Hrnčíř and Klacek (1991) on the Czech and Slovak Republic, and Berg and Sachs (1992), Gomulka (1992), and Calvo and Coricelli (1992) on Poland. The emphasis here is on identifying trends that relate to the credibility of policy, so that the analysis can be related to capital flight. Because the data period is so short and relates to a time in which economic conditions were highly unstable, the results of this exercise should be interpreted with care.

The appendix contains details of the methods and data sources used to estimate capital flight. Table 5.1 reports for the figures for Poland and Table 5.2 the figures for the Czech and Slovak Republic.

Casual observation presents a confused picture. The early stages of transition have shown a tendency for both countries to experience capital outflows. The volume was much greater for Poland in the first year of its transition, but it appeared to have reversed the outflow by 1992 while the Czech and Slovak Republic was still experiencing sizeable outflows. Given the high proportion of foreign currency deposits held domestically in Poland (at the start of the transition process more than 50 percent of money was held in foreign currency), it is not surprising to see a decline, but there remains a large share (around 25 percent). In the case of the Czech and Slovak Republic, the movement has been the reverse (at the start of the transition process the proportion was around 3 percent), but still a much smaller proportion of

TABLE 5.1 Estimate of Capital Flight from Poland and Related Information 1990–92 (US$ million)

	CUDCF1	*CUDCF2*	*WBCF*	*BISCF*	*PSNFA*	*FCD*
1990	8	62	3802	210	1499	31.7%
1991	828	1084	662	90	1543	24.7%
1992	353	102	-1064	70	1013	24.8%

where:

CUDCF1 = Cuddington measure (all currencies);
CUDCF2 = Cuddington measure (convertible currencies);
WBCF = World Bank measure;
BISCF = Change in foreign currency deposits of domestic residents, at BIS area banks;
PSNFA = Change in net foreign assets of the private sector;
FCD = Ratio of domestic foreign currency holdings to total money supply (quasi-money).

TABLE 5.2 Estimates of Capital Flight from the Czech and Slovak Federal Republic and Related Information 1991–92 (US$ million)

	CUDCF1	*CUDCF2*	*WBCF*	*BISCF*	*PSNFA*	*FCD*
1991	-81	-583	1456	1441	1424	6%
1992	171	687	1936	N/A	N/A	10.8%

Note: See Table 5.1 for variable definitions

foreign currency is held than in Poland. In order to relate these figures to policy credibility it is necessary to review the macroeconomic developments in both countries.

Poland entered the transition process with a very large inherited hard currency debt (about $45 billion). The monetary overhang had been eroded substantially by hyperinflation in 1989, but there was still significant inflationary potential. Exchange rate policy involved a move to current account convertibility and the adoption of a pegged exchange rate following a significant over-devaluation which increased the competitiveness of Polish industry. This generated a current account surplus after the "big bang," but there was a deterioration during late 1991 and 1992, reflecting the increase in the real exchange rate. While there was a budget surplus in the early stages of the reform process, the increase in unemployment and the sharp drop in output generated a shift into deficit which continued to increase during 1992.

The Polish macroeconomic developments illustrate the considerable problems faced by policymakers. Stabilization of the economy proved more difficult than the early economic developments suggested. The political process did not aid the building of policy credibility. Polish governments have frequently come and gone, although the election of the Sukhova government in June 1992 created stability during the remainder of the period we examine (note that political instability is again a problem in 1993–94). The overall picture must have looked risky to potential investors, and the path of foreign direct investment confirms that it is only in the second half of 1992 that economic and political conditions became more favorable and led to significant inflows (a 1992 report by Business International/Creditanstalt emphasizes how political uncertainty reduces foreign direct investment). It should be noted, however, that the figures for foreign direct investment tend to understate the total because they ignore a significant number of joint ventures.

Taking the capital flight estimates for Poland as a whole, we can infer that capital flight in the region of US$1 to 3 billion has taken place. Given the macroeconomic uncertainty this may not seem to be a very large figure, but it is important to bear in mind that the legality of holding foreign currency deposits domestically will have stemmed the leakage of capital abroad.[23] Hence, while some flight does seem to have taken place, the high positive nominal interest rates (saving deposit rates rose to 80 percent in 1991 and declined to around 40 percent by the third quarter of 1992 and have fallen only slowly since then) and the apparent commitment of the Polish government to reform has prevented larger outflows.

The data for the Czech and Slovak Republic, where there was only a small hard currency debt (which was almost matched by hard currency assets) and the key macro-policy variables were in good shape, supports the analysis of the Polish case. The budget deficit was not a significant problem, although it has recently shown some deterioration, while the improvement in the current account during the transition process is quite marked. This resulted from the major improvement in competitiveness which resulted from the large devaluation of the Czechoslovak koruna in early 1991. The path of inflation has enhanced the credibility of the pegged exchange rate policy, and has been a significant stabilizing factor. The collapse in industrial output is similar to that in Poland and reflects the need for reallocation of resources, the result of the adoption of a free-market price structure, and the effects of the stabilization policy. Unemployment has not increased as much as in Poland, but this may be a result of disguised unemployment, particularly in the agricultural sector, rather than some underlying difference in the two economies. The overall picture of relatively stable macroeconomic conditions in the Czech and Slovak Republic appears to be borne out by the quite large, and increasing, amounts of foreign direct investment.

Clearly capital flight has not taken place to the same extent in the Czech and Slovak Republic as in Poland, although it should be borne in mind that Poland is roughly twice the size in terms of economic output. However, the move into foreign currency deposits by residents of the Czech and Slovak

Republic is consistent with a general desire to place purchasing power into foreign currencies, even in an economy which has been markedly more successful in producing stable macroeconomic conditions. This behavior can be explained by taking into account the political uncertainty. During the early stages of transition, the Czech and Slovak Republic was dogged by the move towards a separation into the Czech Republic and Slovakia. These political developments clearly created conditions in which it was likely that some capital flight would occur. Note that the $687 million value in 1992 for capital flight includes $535 million in the fourth quarter. At the time this was written, the evidence for 1993 seemed to suggest that the split of the country has been more beneficial to the Czech Republic in terms of key macroeconomic indicators. The importance of political factors in generating capital flight has already been documented for the Latin American economies (Alesina and Tabellini 1989).

Exchange Rate Policy, Capital Flight and Economic Transformation: Policy Conclusions

In the previous section we examined evidence of capital flight in Poland and the Czech and Slovak Republic, and we attempted to provide an explanation for the patterns observed. In this final section potential policy conclusions arising from this analysis are presented.

Restricted convertibility has not prevented significant capital outflows from Poland and, to some extent, the Czech and Slovak Republic. Some of this can be attributed to normal portfolio diversification in the absence of well-developed domestic financial markets, instruments, and institutions. However, the experiences of both Poland and the Czech and Slovak Republic suggest that at least part of the outflow represents capital flight.

The more difficult initial macroeconomic circumstances in Poland relative to the Czech and Slovak Republic do appear to have generated much additional capital flight, and the foreign direct investment flows indicate that there has been some impact. In addition, political uncertainty seems to have been a significant cause of the unfavorable patterns observed in both economies. If this is true, then increasingly stable political environments will be beneficial.

What particular features of policy can affect the perceived risks of holding domestic assets? The following are offered as suggestions.

1. An initial undervaluation of the exchange rate assists in establishing a credible exchange rate peg, which can potentially serve as a nominal anchor, once prices have adjusted to eliminate shortages and reduce devaluation risk.

2. The control of budget deficits and wage increases are important in establishing credibility, and it is the prospect of future control which is vital to this process.
3. Ensuring that real interest rates are positive will not only encourage the retention of capital domestically, but also the repatriation of capital which has already flown. The early launch of privatization and government borrowing programs (especially via the Euromarkets) will also encourage repatriation if recent experiences in Latin American countries can be taken as a guide (World Bank 1993).
4. Macroeconomic stability is important, but political stability with a commitment to stabilization is also necessary to stop capital flight. There is clearly an important link between the credibility of the macroeconomic stabilization program and political stability, but the independent influence of the political process should not be underestimated.

Lessons can also be learned from the analysis of the decision to move to full currency convertibility. The significant capital flight identified in the case of Poland does suggest that the benefits of retaining controls over the movement of funds abroad may be overestimated when the incentives for engaging in that activity are large. However, it is not reasonable to suppose that the controls have no effect, particularly in the early stages of the transition process when macroeconomic conditions are very volatile. The question which should be posed is: "What are the benefits of moving to a fully convertible currency?" Essentially, the argument is the same as applied to the case for liberalizing trade in goods: namely that exposing domestic producers (i.e., banks) to foreign competition will assist in the transformation process.[24] Against this, there is the (infant industry) case for adopting limited (e.g. current account) convertibility to allow the domestic financial system time to develop so that it has a fair chance to compete on equal terms.

Three factors need to be resolved before the financial system is in a position to compete. First, the banking system must be relieved of its inherited debt problem which has clearly prevented it from developing along market-orientated lines. This has major fiscal consequences, which could affect the credibility of the whole reform process. But the experience of the transition process in both Poland and the Czech and Slovak Republic has demonstrated that this problem must be tackled at some stage and that sooner is less costly than later, by which time banks may well have made the problem worse by further misallocation of credit (Dickinson 1992). One possible way of solving the problem would be to write off the debts while creating future tax liabilities against the banking system as a whole. Writing off bank debts also has a beneficial impact on the privatization process through the reduction of enterprises' indebtedness (Mullineux 1992b, 1994), and will assist in the identification of winners and losers among enterprises (Calvo and Frenkel 1991). This leads neatly into the second requirement, which is for the privatization program to be underway with a clear schedule for its completion. This is important for the move to full convertibility so as to provide domestically for the sort of portfolio diversification which might otherwise generate significant capital outflows, and to create the opportunity of generating inward flows (repatriation) of flight capital to balance outflows resulting from the diversification process (World Bank 1993). The third requirement is for proper and comprehensive bankruptcy laws to be in place.

How soon could Poland and the Czech Republic consider a move to full convertibility? The evidence presented above, with the added observation that the privatization process is well underway in the Czech Republic and is accelerating in Poland, points towards the possibility of a fairly early move to full convertibility.[25] This might seem rather hasty, but it is important to realize that the failure to achieve a "big bang" in the financial sector has retarded the transition process and increased the costs involved. The time frame may be longer for Poland, but it is important that a proper plan is put in place so that institutions know in which direction they are headed and can respond accordingly. Competition from financial institutions outside of domestic borders, or the expectation of it, will have a significant beneficial impact on the transformation process and to delay unduly will only increase the transition costs.

What lessons can be drawn from the experiences of Poland and the Czech and Slovak Republic for other emerging market economies at an earlier stage in their transition programs? Firstly, the introduction of current account convertibility seems to enhance the credibility of the reform package, has aided restructuring, and encouraged export reorientation. Secondly, it was correct to restrict capital account convertibility to foreigners initially. To attract foreign capital to assist in the transition, both from a funding point of view and to facilitate transfer of "know-how" or skills and new technology, it is necessary to allow repatriation of profits and capital in foreign exchange. There is also a risk of large-scale capital outflows, as residents diversify their portfolios by purchasing financial assets which are not yet available in the rudimentary domestic financial system, even if internationally competitive interest rates are offered by banks. Further, if the monetary overhang is not completely eliminated by inflation prior to the establishment of convertibility, there is an added risk that capital will be moved overseas to avoid the inflation tax. To the extent that foreign exchange controls can contain capital flight, however, it may be possible to absorb at least some of the "overhang" via the early launch of privatization programs and the issue of government bonds. This would provide alternative financial assets (to bank deposits) and may prevent accumulated "forced saving" being spent on consumer goods and thereby driving up prices. It would also encourage repatriation of capital that has already "flown." Further, special tax exemptions to foreign investors should be limited as they encourage "round tripping" by potential domestic investors.

Even if foreign exchange controls are maintained, there is a risk of capital flight via misinvoicing. To deal with this and leakages in the foreign exchange controls, it is necessary to reduce the incentive for capital flight. This entails establishing a credible exchange rate policy with a domestic rate of return that compensates adequately for inflation and devaluation risks and encourages the development of financial markets. Given the high level of uncertainty associated with transition economies, the risk of capital flight, and the need for governments to acquire "reputation," it is probable that an "overtight" monetary policy, with higher interest rates than might otherwise be required, will be needed. Such a policy would be overtight in the sense that it would be tighter than strictly required to achieve inflation convergence with trading partners. The transition recession would consequently be aggravated (Calvo and Coricelli 1992). It is not obvious that the foreign exchange markets will allow a policy of deliberate "undervaluation," but Poland and the Czech and Slovak Republic seem to have achieved this and it is clear that a policy of sustained overvaluation would aggravate the problem. Overreliance on high interest rates to achieve stabilization is anyway dangerous given the inherited debt overhang in the state-owned enterprise sector.

Once relieved of their debt burdens, banks could assist in the restructuring process by performing their credit allocation, "monitoring," and perhaps wider corporate governance roles (Belka and Mullineux 1993) without being subject to the "perverse" incentives (Begg and Portes 1992) which perpetuate resource misallocation. If the debt problem is not resolved at the outset, monetary restraint, and high interest rates in particular, are likely to lead to a distortionary restructuring (Begg 1991). In Poland and the Czech and Slovak Republic, monetary restraint was pursued using a combination of mildly positive real interest rates and credit ceilings backed by reserve requirements. The latter allowed interest rates to be kept at levels that did not aggravate the debt problem excessively. In order to circumvent the bank lending restrictions, however, firms extended interenterprise credits to each other in the early phases of the transition. Monetary policy appears, therefore, to have been fairly lax *de facto*. In Poland's case, this is disputed by Calvo and Coricelli (1992), who argue that the policy was in fact initially "overtight." The relatively low real interest rates and apparent laxity in monetary restraint perhaps accounts for the acceptance by the foreign currency markets of "undervaluation" and for the persistence of "post bang" inflation. Calvo and Coricelli (1991) explain the persistence of inflation by a relaxation of the initially "overtight" monetary policy in the second half of

1990. From the point of view of foreign exchange traders, however, the currencies were clearly correctly valued, in the light of the relative interest rate being offered on zloty or koruna bank deposits and the risks involved. Some initial "undervaluation" is anyway required to allow for the upward price level adjustment necessary to eliminate shortages following the removal of subsidies and following the introduction of VAT.

To enhance credibility and reduce the need to have an "overtight" monetary policy, a currency board, as in Estonia, and/or central bank independence could also be introduced. The establishment of an "independent" central bank may be desirable in the longer run, but is unlikely to enhance credibility in the early stages of transition, since the central bank must itself acquire a reputation as an inflation fighter and is likely to try to do so by maintaining an "overtight" monetary policy.

It is not clear that a currency board is consistent with the Western-style fractional reserve banking systems which the transition economies are trying, and indeed being advised, to establish (Bofinger 1992, Section 6.3.1.). The move to fractional reserve banking would entail bank credit being accepted as money alongside central bank liabilities, even though it is not backed by foreign exchange reserves. Under a currency board with fractional reserve banking, there would be limited lender-of-last-resort cover because the central bank cannot expand its liabilities until it acquires more foreign exchange. This could undermine confidence in the banking system and convertibility. As noted above, the state-owned banks in the transition economies tend to be undercapitalized and have substantial bad debts. However, because they are state-backed and continue to dominate the financial system, they may have to be bailed out to avoid economic collapse. The restricted lender-of-last-resort cover is also likely to be a major deterrent to the development of private sector banks, which would have to compete with state-owned, and perhaps implicitly state-guaranteed, banks.

The problem is again one of lack of credibility. Under fractional reserve banking, even 100 percent foreign exchange backing for central bank liabilities would be insufficient to guarantee the credibility of the currency board. If depositors lost confidence they would have an incentive to cash in deposits and buy foreign currency, and "runs" would therefore take the form of capital flight. Foreign exchange controls could reduce the risk, but the incentive will remain in the absence of credibility and the currency board is unlikely to enhance it. It will be interesting to compare the medium-term experiences of Argentina, which in 1991 introduced a currency board system along with central bank independence to support an overvalued exchange rate, and whose subsequent growth and inflation performance has been remarkable; with Poland and the Czech and Slovak Republic, which introduced central bank independence and adopted undervalued exchange rates; and Estonia, which only started its transition in June 1992. It introduced a currency board with an undervalued exchange rate, along with central bank independence. It should be noted that a currency stabilization fund is likely to enhance the credibility of the exchange rate target following the introduction of convertibility whether a currency board is adopted or not. For this reason such funds were provided for Poland and the Czech and Slovak Republic, as noted above.

Finally, to avoid the need to undervalue prior to credibly fixing the exchange rate for a protracted period, a crawling peg devaluation might be advisable (Bomhoff 1992). To avoid overreliance on domestic monetary restraint, a strict wages policy would be a useful adjunct (Bomhoff 1992; Calvo and Coricelli 1992). The ability to impose a strict wages policy without the help of a nominal anchor in the form of a fixed nominal exchange rate will depend on political factors. This was evident in Poland, where the big bang was introduced while control of the state-owned enterprises remained largely in the hands of workers' councils. The political acceptability of the program was probably related to the hyperinflationary experience that preceded its introduction. Hyperinflation may have made the public more willing to accept austerity in Argentina, too. In neither case has inflation been eradicated, and there has been increasing evidence in both countries since the second half of 1992 that the public, or significant sections of it, are becoming "disenchanted" with the austerity. The Czech and Slovak Republic, and now the Czech Republic, seems to be different. Its traditional fiscal and monetary conservatism and willingness to partially relieve the debt problem (Begg 1991) at a relatively early stage has led to a reassertion of the reform program under ex-Finance Minister, and now Prime Minister, Vaclav Klaus.

Appendix: Calculating Capital Flight

The data are taken from a variety of sources including the IMF *Balance of Payments Yearbook*, IMF *International Financial Statistics* and Plan Econ *Country Reports*. The measures of capital flight reported are:

Cuddington (*CUDCF*): (1) short-term private sector capital flows; (2) errors and omissions. *CUDCF1* reports the value for all currencies (IMF, *Balance of Payments Yearbook*) while *CUDCF2* reports the value for convertible currencies based on errors and omissions (IMF, *International Financial Statistics*).

World Bank (*WBCF*):

Change in Debt + Current Account + Net FDI
+ Change in Reserves (an increase is negative)

The size of hard currency debt is reported at the gross level (from Plan Econ *Country Reports*). To convert this to net official debt, the capital account balance of the official sector (from *International Financial Statistics*) is deducted from the gross figure. The current account and net foreign direct investment figures are from Plan Econ *Country Reports,* while the change in reserves is the sum of the change in reserve assets (Czech National Bank) plus official financing (from *International Financial Statistics*). Note that net foreign direct investment is likely to be underreported for these countries.

BIS Deposits (*BISCF*): Change in deposits, held by domestic residents, in BIS area commercial banks (from Plan Econ *Country Reports*).

Banking System and Private Sectors' Foreign Assets (*PSNFA*): Change in net foreign asset position of the commercial banking system and private sector (from *International Financial Statistics*).

Domestic Holding of Foreign Currency Deposits (*FCD*): Expressed as the ratio between the foreign currency component of domestic money supply and total quasi-money (from Plan Econ *Country Reports* and *International Financial Statistics*).

It has not been possible to report all figures for both countries because of data unavailability.

Notes

Financial support from the French State Planning Commission for research on which this paper is based is gratefully acknowledged.

1. Since January 1993 this has been two separate countries: the Czech Republic and the Slovak Republic.
2. The causes of capital inflows (foreign direct investment and portfolio investment) are not investigated in detail, hence the emphasis on causes of gross capital outflows.
3. See Greene and Isard (1991) for a more detailed discussion.
4. See Asselian (1991), Bofinger (1991), Bomhoff (1992) and Polak (1991).
5. In fact, they argue that any outflow is bad for a capital-starved economy.
6. See Cumby and Levich (1987).
7. It has been estimated that up to 60 percent of currency was in the form of dollars at the start of the Polish reform process. This introduces the issue of currency substitution, which is closely related to the analysis of capital flight. In particular, residents can satisfy their desire for currency diversification by holding foreign currency deposits domestically. However, this does not deal with expropriation risk, which may be the major cause of capital flight. For a survey of models of currency substitution see Giovannini and Turtelboom (1992).
8. In Poland the business sector gave up dollars when their access to credit was

restricted in 1991 while households were eventually induced to give up dollars because banks offered much higher rates of interest on zloty accounts.

9. Which was a major problem in Russia in 1992.

10. Prior to the introduction of "the reforms," a monobanking system prevailed. Then, typically in the late 1980s, a two-tier system was created by separating central banking functions from commercial banking functions, which were to be performed by a number of "commercial" banks. The latter were newly created state-owned institutions or existing state-owned, formerly "specialized" banks, and were usually organized on a (industrial) sectoral or regional basis. See Corbett and Mayer (1991).

11. This is particularly true if VAT is to be introduced.

12. Witness the Russian experience of February 1991, when the largest denomination notes were withdrawn from circulation, and in August 1993, when a more comprehensive currency reform was introduced by the central bank but watered down by President Yeltsin.

13. Some studies have tackled the issue of policy credibility during a major reform process, e.g. Baxter (1985) and Rodrik (1989).

14. In a similar vein Agenor and Taylor (1992) argue that the transitory component of the parallel market foreign exchange premium can be used to measure credibility.

15. Van Wijnbergen (1985) has developed a theoretical analysis of the credibility of trade policy reforms and capital flight.

16. Capital inflows can, of course, cause domestic currency appreciation and this, of itself, can create policy credibility problems (Morande 1988).

17. The literature on country risk, developed to analyze international lending, also emphasizes the importance of political risk (e.g. see Eaton, Gersovitz and Stiglitz 1986).

18. Note that a recent survey (Business International/Creditanstalt 1992) has emphasized the importance of "political risk" to foreign investors when considering direct investment into Eastern Europe.

19. This has seemed to be a characteristic of successful Latin American stabilizations (Végh 1992).

20. Commodity convertibility refers to the right of enterprises to use bank balances to purchase goods without "planning permission." It is sometimes used more broadly to encompass the rights of households to freely use money to acquire goods, and of enterprises to sell goods at their own discretion, rather than to a purchaser identified by the planner.

21. See Hrnčíř and Klacek (1991) for further discussion.

22. The ability of capital controls to restrict capital flight is an open question (see Phylaktis 1988). Note also that currency substitution may be a major problem when internal convertibility is adopted (Rogers 1992).

23. Although there would still be the risk of a sudden policy reversal to counteract, this does not seem to have been too significant.

24. The rationales for capital controls and benefits to be expected from easing them are discussed in detail in Mathieson and Rojas-Suárez (1993).

25. The plan in the Czech and Slovak Republics is, at present, to go fully convertible in 1996.

References

Agenor, Pierre-Richard, and Mark P. Taylor. 1992. "Testing for Credibility Effects." *IMF Staff Papers* 39: 545–71.

Alesina, Albert, and Guido Tabellini. 1989. "External Debt, Capital Flight and Political Risk." *Journal of International Economics* 27: 199–220.

Asselian, J. C. 1991. "Convertibility and Economic Transformation." *European Economy,* Special Issue No. 2, June: 215–41.

Baxter, Mariann. 1985. "The Role of Expectations in Stabilization Policy." *Journal of Monetary Economics* 15: 343–62

Begg, David. 1991. "Economic Reform in the Czech and Slovak Republic: Should We Believe in Santa Klaus?" *Economic Policy* 13: 244–86.

Begg, David, and Richard Portes. 1992. "Enterprise Debt and Economic Transformation: Financial Restructuring of the State Sector in Central and Eastern Europe." *CEPR Discussion Paper* No. 695. London: Centre for Economic Policy Research.

Belka, Marek, and Andrew W. Mullineux. 1993. "Hardening Micro Budget Constraints: Bank Behaviour and Corporate Governance in Poland." International Finance Groups Working Paper 93-08, University of Birmingham.

Berg, Andrew, and Jeffrey Sachs. 1992. "Structural Adjustment and International Trade in Eastern Europe: The Case of Poland." *Economic Policy* 14: 118–73.

Bofinger, Peter. 1991. "Options for the Payments and Exchange Rate System in Eastern Europe." *European Economy,* Special Issue No. 2, June: 243–61.

Bomhoff, Eduard J. 1992. "Monetary Reform in Eastern Europe." *European Economic Review* 36: 454–58.

Business International/Creditanstalt. 1992. "East European Investment Survey." Vienna, October.

Calvo, Guillermo, and Fabrizio Coricelli. 1992. "Stabilization in Poland." *Economic Policy*, April: 176–226.

Calvo, Guillermo, and Jacob A. Frenkel. 1991. "Credit Markets, Credibility and Economic Transformation." *Journal of Economic Perspectives* 5: 139–48.

Corbett, Jenny, and Colin Mayer. 1991. "Financial Reform in Eastern Europe: Progress with the Wrong Model." *Oxford Review of Economic Policy* 7(4): 57–75.

Cuddington, John T. 1986. "Capital Flight: Estimates, Issues and Explanations." *Princeton Studies in International Finance* No. 58. Princeton, N.J.: International Finance Section, Princeton University.

———. 1987. "Macroeconomic Determinants of Capital Flight: An Empirical Investigation," in Donald R. Lessard and John Williamson, eds., *Capital Flight and Third World Debt.* Pp. 85–95. Washington, D.C.: Institute for International Economics.

Cumby, Robert, and Richard Levich. 1987. "On the Definitions and Magnitude of Recent Capital Flight," in Donald R. Lessard and John Williamson, eds., *Capital Flight and Third World Debt.* Pp. 27–67. Washington, D.C.: Institute for International Economics.

Dickinson, David G. 1992. "Some Aspects of Banking Risk." *International Finance Group Working Paper*, University of Birmingham.

Dooley, Michael P. 1987. "Capital Flight: A Response to Differences in Risks." *IMF Staff Papers* 35: 422–36.
Eaton, Jonathan, Mark Gersovitz and Joseph E. Stiglitz. 1986. "The Pure Theory of Country Risk." *European Economic Review* 30: 481–513.
Giovannini, Alberto, and Bart Turtelboom. 1992. "Currency Substitution." *NBER Working Paper* No. 4232. Cambridge, Mass.: National Bureau of Economic Research, December.
Gomulka, Stanislaw. 1992. "Polish Economic Reform 1990–91: Principles, Policies and Outcomes." *Cambridge Journal of Economics* 16: 355–72.
Greene, Joshua E., and Peter Isard. 1991. "Currency Convertibility and the Transformation of Centrally Planned Economies." *IMF Occasional Paper* No. 81. Washington D.C.: International Monetary Fund.
Gulati, Sunil K. 1987. "A Note on Trade Misinvoicing," in Donald R. Lessard and John Williamson, eds., *Capital Flight and Third World Debt.* Pp. 68–78. Washington, D.C.: Institute for International Economics.
Hrnčíř, Miroslav, and Jan Klacek. 1991. "Stabilization Policies and Currency Convertibility in Czechoslovakia." *European Economy*, Special Issue, June: 17–39.
Khan, Mohsin S., and Nadeem Ul Haque. 1985. "Foreign Borrowing and Capital Flight: A Formal Analysis." *IMF Staff Papers* 32: 606–28.
Kornai, Janos. 1990. *The Road to a Free Economy: Shifting from a Socialist Economy. The Example of Hungary.* New York: W.W. Norton.
Lessard, Donald R., and John Williamson. 1987. *Capital Flight and Third World Debt.* Washington, D.C.: Institute for International Economics.
Morande, Felipe G. 1988. "Domestic Currency Appreciation and Foreign Capital Inflows: What Comes First? (Chile, 1977–82)." *Journal of International Money and Finance* 7: 447–66.
Markowitz, Harry M. 1991. *Portfolio Selection,* 2nd ed. Oxford: Basil Blackwell.
Mathieson, Donald, and Liliana Rojas-Suárez. 1993. "Liberalization of the Capital Account: Experiences and Issues." *IMF Occasional Paper* No. 103. Washington D.C.: International Monetary Fund.
Mullineux, Andrew W. 1992a. "Hard Budget Constraints, Credit Crunches and Central Bank Independence." *University of Wales Business and Economics Review* 8: 35–8.
———. 1992b. "Privatization and Financial Structure in Eastern and Central European Countries." National Westminster Bank *Quarterly Review*, May: 12–25.
———. 1994. "Banks, Privatization and Restructuring in Poland." *University of Wales Business and Economics Review* 9: 38–45.
Phylaktis, Kate. 1988. "Capital Controls: The Case of Argentina." *Journal of International Money and Finance* 7: 303–20.
Polak, Jacques J. 1991. "Convertibility: An Indispensable Element in the Transition Process in Eastern Europe," in John Williamson, ed., *Currency Convertibility in Eastern Europe*. Pp. 21–30. Washington, D.C.: Institute for International Economics.
Portes, Richard. 1992. "Structural Reform in Central and Eastern Europe." *European Economic Review* 36: 661–69.
Rodrik, Dani. 1989. "Promises, Promises: Credible Policy Reform via Signalling." *Economic Journal* 99: 756–72.

Rodriguez, Miguel A. 1987. "Consequences of Capital Flight for Latin American Debtor Countries," in Donald R. Lessard and John Williamson, eds., *Capital Flight and Third World Debt.* Pp. 129–44. Washington, D.C.: Institute for International Economics.

Rogers, John H. 1992. "Convertibility Risk and Dollarisation in Mexico: A Vector Autoregressive Analysis." *Journal of International Money and Finance* 11: 188–207.

Rojas-Suárez, Liliana. 1991. "Risk and Capital Flight in Developing Countries," in *Determinants and Systemic Consequences of International Capital Flows.* IMF Occasional Paper No. 77. Pp. 83–92. Washington, D.C.: International Monetary Fund.

Van Wijnbergen, Sweder. 1985. "Trade Reform, Aggregate Investment and Capital Flight." *Economics Letters* 19: 369–72.

Végh, Carlos. 1992. "Stopping High Inflation: An Analytical Overview." *IMF Staff Papers*, September: 626–95.

Williamson, John. 1991. *The Economic Opening of Eastern Europe*. Washington D.C.: Institute for International Economics.

Williamson, John, and Donald R. Lessard. 1987. *Capital Flight: The Problem and Policy Responses*. Washington, D.C.: Institute for International Economics.

World Bank. 1993. "Global Economic Prospects and Developing Countries." Washington D.C.: International Bank for Reconstruction and Development.

Yuravlivker, David E. 1987. "Political Shocks, International Reserves and the Real Exchange Rate." *Journal of International Money and Finance* 6: 401–17.

6

Capital Controls and Corporate Investment Behavior

Christine P. Ries

Introduction

In Chapter 2 of this book, Manuel Guitián reviews the role of controls on capital flows in the postwar development of the global economy. In essence, he suggests that government attempts to restrict capital flows, either by restricting rates of return or erecting barriers to the flow of capital, fall within the "international financial code of conduct" established after World War II. Such financial code of conduct norms were established at Bretton Woods in response to the central challenge of the time—"to insure the integration of war-ridden and restricted economies into an orderly international economic system."[1] On the surface, the challenge of providing for an orderly integration of the economies of formerly communist countries into the global economic system may seem similar in character to that of the postwar problem.

This chapter accepts the challenge of integration, but rejects the assumption that capital controls are the most effective policy prescription for the achievement of this objective. Basic elements of the global economy and global social structure have changed so dramatically since the 1950s that the prescriptions of that time are not only outmoded for today, but are potentially destructive. At a minimum, national policymakers must consider a number of more pervasive though indirect consequences of capital controls. These include effects on national comparative advantage and on industrial and ownership patterns of the future.

The international policy norms adopted at the end of World War II were based on a vision of a world economic system that consisted of relatively independent, sovereign nations. The ability of each regime to offer independent and autonomous social and economic policies was to be protected and prosperity was to be provided from within. Economic integration was to be accomplished primarily through international trade in goods and commodities. The need for capital controls to protect this vision, especially with respect to retaining national policy autonomy, was necessarily accepted and acceptable. In the immediate postwar period, the assumption of policy independence and autonomy may have been reasonable.

Assumptions of independence and autonomy in today's environment are no longer tenable, however. Capital controls ultimately depend on the government's ability to *suppress demand* for a broad range of investment alternatives. Since at least the late 1970s, however, governments have found it increasingly difficult to suppress and deny the demands of savers, investors and borrowers for access to the broader range of investment and risk management products.

This explosion in demand for a variety of investment securities and for access to global capital markets has been stimulated and facilitated by tremendous advances in our abilities to access and analyze information. New technologies have stimulated demand for access to opportunities of all types including demands for new and expanded forms of employment opportunity, demands for more education and information, and even for new and more effective forms of government. In the face of these demands, governments are no longer in a position to successfully restrict access to such instruments of prosperity as education, information, and access to capital markets. Increasingly, political and social stability requires that governments facilitate institutions that support increasing prosperity, improved employment opportunities, security, and the accumulation of wealth. Further, opportunities for progress and increased standards of well-being are no longer considered absolute, but are judged by electorates in relation to the living standards in other countries. Finally prosperity, relative or absolute, can no longer be generated solely within national borders, but must rely on fully functioning interface with the global economic and social systems.

This essay demonstrates that capital controls represent an attempt to destroy linkages between national and global systems and that those linkages are essential to the creation and maintenance of national prosperity. Further, while the initial impact will certainly be negative, it is the longer term impact that will be the largest and potentially most destabilizing.

While it is true that national governments may still have some ability to manage rates of returns to capital and the volume of cross-border capital flows, it is less and less certain that a regime can achieve its objectives by exercising such control. Rather, attempts to manage the flow of capital into preferred industries or sectors and with preferred distribution effects will affect the development of national industrial structure and ownership patterns in many unforeseen and undesirable ways. Distortions in investment and ownership patterns created by capital controls are similar to the distortions in efficiency and distribution that result from attempts to protect various sectors by restricting competition.

This chapter describes the effects of capital controls on a nation's ability to achieve an efficient allocation of existing capital resources and to attract new capital investment. The analysis exposes the bias in ownership structure that accompanies capital controls and shows that this bias in the ownership of private enterprise becomes politically unstable over time.

These arguments lead to the conclusion that restrictive policies will obstruct rather than facilitate the transition to an efficient and globally competitive national economy. While such restrictions appear to protect domestic interests, in reality they exclude domestic producers and investors from access to essential information about the operation of the global economy. The short-term effects on the ability to attract and allocate capital will be significant, and the long-term destruction of the ability of national investors and producers to compete in a global economy is potentially disastrous.

The relationship between capital controls, the future competitiveness of national companies, and prosperity is developed below in series of steps. The next section frames the arguments with respect to a single policy objective—providing economic growth and prosperity. It demonstrates that the attraction and allocation of capital are prime ingredients in the achievement of this policy goal. The third section describes the roles of capital markets and investor analysis in the attraction and allocation of capital and recognizes the importance of location and other factors. In this context, we review the basic elements of investment analysis that will determine the outcome of the selection decision. We focus specifically on the role of the *discount rate* in the investment analysis and show its impact on the magnitude of aggregate investment and on investment allocation across sectors and over time. In the following section we consider the impact of capital controls on the discount rate and demonstrate that controls affect local and foreign investors differently. This section presents a review of the prescriptions of modern portfolio theory and offers us important insights into the relationship between increases in risk and increases in investors' required returns. It is the essence of these theories and perspectives that present a major challenge to those who would include capital controls as an element of growth policy.

We then review the implications of the discount rate effects for the foundations of the national economy. By acting on the discount rate structure, capital controls affect the proportions of capital and labor, the structure of national industry and ownership, population migration patterns and future national competitiveness. The final section summarizes the effects of capital controls on the economy, in general, and on the relative economic position of the local population relative to foreign owners and managers. Implications for political stability are significant.

Achieving Economic Prosperity

Economic growth and prosperity require the *efficient allocation* of *sufficient amounts* of capital resources. Much has been written elsewhere about the many essential institutional underpinnings that promote the attraction and efficient allocation of capital. These include institutions that support the development and protection of property rights, support private contracting initiatives, and regulatory and governance systems that encourage growth while preserving fairness and equity.[2]

To attract investment a nation must provide attractive opportunities for returns in the future. In addition to assessing the importance of providing an environment that increases the probability of future success, national policy must recognize direct competition from other governments that are also attempting to attract capital. In this chapter, I describe the investment analysis and decision from the perspective of the investor so that policy analysts may evaluate the effects of capital controls and other policies on future investment success. The approach recognizes that the investor is essentially purchasing both a political and geographic site. This perspective allows us to recognize essential elements of national advantage and of public policies that influence the investor's choice of one site over another.

The approach also allows us to relate current investment requirements to future rewards and thereby demonstrate the connection between the amount of capital attracted and investors' expectations of the probability of future economic growth and social stability.

In summary, I adopt the perspective of the investor to examine the factors that will either promote or retard the commitment of capital in a particular national setting, and given existing national physical and social endowments. My interest is in the essential underpinnings for economic growth: increasing capital resources and improving the allocation of that capital.

Investment Valuation and the Investment Location Decision

A Model of Investment Valuation

From the perspective of an investor, a particular location's investment value depends on the pattern of cash flows that site can be expected to generate. The realization of each expectation depends on any number of contingencies, unknown in the present. The levels of these uncertainties together with the expected return itself, are the two essential determinants of the present value of the investment opportunity. Those uncertainties, or risk, are captured in a discount rate, which is directly related to the level of risk.[3] The higher the risk, the higher the discount rate and the lower the present value of any given expected future receipt. In essence, the discount rate translates the expectation of a future receipt into an initial present investment amount. This amount is the cash equivalent of a bet on the future opportunity. The greater the risk of the bet, the larger the discount.

In a general form, the value of an investment that will generate future returns is the sum of those discounted expected future cash flows:

$$V = \Sigma \mathrm{E}\,(CF_t)/\,(1 + COC)^t \qquad (1)$$

where:

V	=	the value of the investment opportunity, i.e., the present value of the future cash flows;
$\mathrm{E}(CF_t)$	=	the expectation of the cash return to the investment in period t;
COC	=	the discount rate that compensates investors for the risk inherent in the project.[4]

In practice, the value of direct investment opportunities is calculated with the application of a full and detailed investment valuation model, with explicit and carefully estimated expectations for future cash flow receipts. That basic form, the value for each particular cash flow, is of the form above. The overall pattern of cash flows is typically an initial outflow, usually in the early periods of the investment, with inflows expected to follow over a longer period of time. Further, the cash flows usually start at some beginning level and increase in size over time.

When we assume that growth occurs at a constant rate over time, equation (1) can be approximated by a very useful abstraction:[5]

$$V = CF/\ COC - g \qquad (2)$$

where:

V	=	the value of the investment opportunity or the present value of the future cash flows;
CF	=	the cash return to the investment in the current period;
COC	=	the discount rate that compensates investors for the risk inherent in the project;
g	=	expected rate of growth of the cash flow.

In this formulation, the value of the investment is determined by the *initial level* of the return, the *expected rate of growth* of returns, and a *discount rate* that reflects the cost of capital, or *risk*, for that investment. Investment values are higher where initial returns are higher, the expected rate of growth is higher, or the risk and the cost of capital is lower.

The present value analysis gives the investor the value of the investment and therefore the maximum price to be paid for that investment. The value captured by the investor is the difference between the discounted present value and the price he is forced to pay for the opportunity. Translated into an international setting where countries compete for investor resources, national policies must recognize that capital is attracted to locations where investment present values exceed investment prices by the greatest differential.[6] Nations that offer investment opportunities with high growth expectations and low risk will be winners in the capital attraction game.

The Basics of Discounting

The cost of capital measures an investor's access to the financial resources required for investment. The fact that the cost of capital is some finite number implies that financing is available at some price. That price, the cost of capital, is the return demanded by the security holders, those who provide the initial investment resources. These investors set the cost of capital, the return that they require in order to justify the commitment of funds, by comparing the risks inherent in the investment opportunity with the risks of other investment alternatives. Private investors willingly supply funds if the return expected from the present opportunity exceeds the return available on other investment opportunities of similar risk. In essence, the rate of return that is required to attract resources to a particular project or investment is determined by investors in comparison to the risk/return tradeoff reflected in the wider marketplace.

This approach highlights the role of the capital markets in resource allocation. By providing for the pricing of risk and trading of investment securities, capital markets facilitate the orderly flow of resources into projects with expected returns that more than compensate investors for the relevant levels of risk. Capital will be denied to investments with future prospects that do not surpass this risk-adjusted return.

Table 6.1 illustrates this effect of discounting on the returns and the cash flow levels required in order to provide positive value and to attract capital. Each cell indicates the discount that is applied to a cash flow to be received at a point in the future, and to which a risk-adjusted discount rate has been applied.

TABLE 6.1 Discount Rates

Cost of Capital	*Year 1*	*Year 2*	*Year 3*	*Year 10*	*Year 20*
10%	.91	.83	.75	**.39**	.15
15%	.87	.76	.66	.25	.06
20%	.83	.69	.58	.16	.03

In other words, the cash to be received ten years hence, and a risk that would command a 10 percent return, is worth only *39* percent of the actual amount to be received in ten years. In order to provide the required rate of return, the expected level of the future cash flows must be sufficiently high to allow for this discounting.

As a simple example, an attractive 10 percent investment of $1000 today must be expected to return at least $2564 in ten years time. The $2564, discounted at 39 percent, just offsets the initial $1000, and the investment yields just 10 percent. For a higher return, or an investment value that exceeds $1000, the future cash flow must exceed $2564.

Table 6.1 also clearly demonstrates the interaction between time and risk. Riskier investments command a higher cost of capital and cash flows are discounted more heavily the longer the time to payoff. Thus, the discounting process takes account of both *time and risk* simultaneously. A project that returns 20 percent is very risky indeed and the promise of a payoff in twenty years is not worth much!

These simple examples of the mechanics of discounting suggest a very powerful framework for the analysis of policies that promote economic growth. Policies that support lower discount rates promote increased investment because the present value of any given investment prospect is larger when the required rate of return is lower and capital is attracted to the support of projects with high current values. Policies that raise the required rates of return for investors, and thereby increase the relevant discount rate, retard the flow of investment capital because fewer projects in the existing pool will be capable of delivering the higher rate of return.

Cash Flow Considerations

There are several other aspects of this formulation that are more financial in nature and arise in the actual application of the formula to the global investment setting. While tangential to the main emphasis on discount rates, a complete assessment of the subject of the effects of regulation and controls on investment valuation requires a discussion of cash flow expectations.

The regulation or restriction of cash flows is one form of controls that has become a staple in the trade policy toolkit. In Chapter 2 of this volume, Guitián describes two forms of restriction. The first type of control restricts the practice of international *financial exchange*. This includes the imposition of dual or multiple exchange rates and differential tax treatment of transactions. The second type of restriction places limits on the *quantity of capital* that may be transferred. Segregation of controls into these two types is reminiscent of the distinction between tariffs and quotas as instruments of international financial policy. Here I briefly assess the former type, exchange restrictions, and reserve the core of my analysis and discussion for limitations on ownership. That is, in this subsection I consider the effects of taxes and regulations on *exchange* and treat the effects of ownership limitations as the main concern of the rest of the chapter.

One common type of exchange restriction is a withholding tax on repatriated earnings or dividends. The commonly used import deposit schemes are yet another type. In this latter case the investor is required to place funds on deposit equal in amount to the cost of imports. Deposits are usually in interest-free or low interest bearing accounts and funds are released from the accounts after a year or more. A similar scheme is sometimes imposed on dividends or profits in order to force retention of profits in the country for an extended period. Again, the funds are usually invested at a lower return than that provided by the operating investment.

These restrictions are recognized in the investment valuation formula as reductions or delays in receipt of expected cash flows. The framework values expected cash flows only when they are available for application to other investment opportunities. In essence, the cash flow must not be required for reinvestment, for growth, for equipment maintenance, etc. The cash must also be "repatriatible." In order to realize full value, the cash flow must be potentially available for application to alternative investments regardless of location, nationality, industry, or other constraint.

Both tax and quota-type restrictions on capital flows are normally enforced with requirements of special approval or negotiated tax assessment. In other words, purchases or sales of foreign assets by domestic residents are prohibited unless administrative authorization for the transaction is received. Securing authorization or approval is a costly process, and often political as well as financial capital must be expended. These costs are reflected as reductions in return and growth.

In addition, the cash flow represents a return after tax and regulatory costs. That is, the cash flow is *net* of any taxes—income or withholding—or any expenses that must be incurred in order to gain the full use of the cash flow.

In cases of transaction restrictions, cash flow growth or timing of receipt are altered unfavorably by controls. With a delay in receipt, forced reinvestment at lower yields or a reduction in *net* cash flow due to taxes or transactions costs reduces the inherent value of the investment opportunity.

As we shall see below, controls that restrict access to certain classes of securities not only share the negative impact on overall value, but also alter the intertemporal allocation of resources.

Investment Valuation and the Economics of Locational Choice

In a competitive and liberal investment market, the prices paid for investment opportunities reflect their value to investors. In a price setting or "buyers" market, opportunities abound for the purchase of investments whose investment value exceeds their price. This is the "capital shortage" environment where there are fewer entrepreneurs than opportunities for productive investment. In this case, when the value of an asset to a particular investor exceeds the price paid for that asset, the investor is said to have "created value." In a market that is more competitive—a seller's market—prices for investment opportunities are bid up by a surplus of entrepreneurs and opportunities to create value are smaller and fewer.

These dynamics have a reverse image from the perspective of the seller, usually the national government or privatization agency. Any excess of proceeds over current value or cost accrues to the seller. In periods of capital shortage, prices paid for investment opportunities are likely to be lower, with more value accruing to the investor. When there is surplus of investors, the prices paid are higher with more of the value created going to the government and relatively less to the investor.

In the absence of taxes or other restrictions on the market for investment opportunities, cash flow expectations and values will reflect locational advantages. The classical theories of trade and economic development have defined advantages in terms of more "natural" factors—access to scarce resources, low-cost factors of production, low-cost labor, or highly skilled labor, large and affluent markets, etc. From this perspective, capital will be attracted to the areas with the highest potential value, that is, with the greatest endowment of these natural factors. In addition, industrial structure will be determined by the match between the types of resources needed in an industry and the resources available locally.

Of course, these traditional theories presume some fixed factor, such as a natural resource or capital endowment, that confers the locational advantage. Most of the theorems of trade and growth derive from the assumption that this locational advantage is geographically fixed or, at least, that it is less than completely mobile.

However, information and export technologies have delivered more complicated and rewarding possibilities for investors who can now use and even create advantages that are increasingly and sometimes completely mobile. For example, with modern information transmission, the product of labor may be completely and instantaneously mobile, even if employees themselves are not.

This mobility of factors implies that, in most cases, productive investment will be attracted more by some *portfolio of endowments* than by some "natural" or *fixed endowment advantage*. These might include access to transportation, a willing and well-trained labor force, a legal and contractual infrastructure, or basic security guarantees. And these endowments are, to some extent, the product of an interaction between the social and economic structure, culture, and government of a nation.[7]

Quite often, these advantages are conferred by an efficient and effective local or national government that provides the immobile infrastructure and legal and governmental institutions that facilitate the efficient and effective operation of business. For example, national governments are increasingly realizing that global investors will not locate in countries that are unable to control crime and provide basic support for business activity.

Factor mobility and technologies that allow investors to combine resources from around the globe have become essential ingredients in competitive success. Investors recognize the importance of this kind of flexibility by placing larger amounts of investment capital and technology in locations where mobility is honored and facilitated. The succeeding sections demonstrate that national policies that attempt to constrain mobility will suffer reduced investor support. Further, policies that constrain capital mobility will also alter the intertemporal allocation of capital in ways that may commit national resources to positions of longer run competitive disadvantage.

Intertemporal Aspects of Discount Rates and Investment Selection

My purpose in this chapter is to consider the effects of capital controls on both the *attraction* and *reallocation* of capital resources. Examples above demonstrated the relationship between discount rates and the amount of capital supplied by investors. In this subsection, I especially review those fundamentals of discounting that determine important aspects of resource allocation.

The level of discount rates is a major determinant of the intertemporal allocation of resources. That is, in addition to determining overall investment attractiveness, discount rates also influence the allocation of funds between programs that are expected to yield returns in the short term (or require expenditures in the short term) and those that offer a longer term payoff (or defer expenditures into the future).

When discount rates are higher, costs and revenues in the future are discounted more heavily and, therefore, have a lower impact on the current value of the project. High discount rates favor the adoption of projects with revenues to be received in the nearer term and with expenditures to be deferred to future periods. Lower discount rates shift investment decisions toward projects that promise higher growth rates relative to present earnings. Lower discount rates also favor investments that expend resources initially in favor of reduced expenditures over the longer term.

In short, when discount rates are lower, projects that require larger initial investment in exchange for future growth are preferred. When discount rates rise, investor preference shifts toward projects that minimize the initial investment and favor short-term over long-term returns.[8]

This relationship between discount rates, initial investment and growth finds a counterpart in classical production economics. In production economics investments are represented as expansions of scale that allow the firm to operate at a lower point on the long-run labor supply curve. An expansion matches the scale of production to the quantity of output in a way that allows an improved combination of factors, potential economies for purchasing in quantity, and increased productivity. Investments in automation are designed to substitute capital for labor or to increase labor productivity in future periods.[9]

From the perspectives of finance and discounting, the capital expansion reflects a decision to invest current resources as a substitute for incurring longer run expenditures. The decision accepts initial investment in exchange for longer term growth. As demonstrated above, this essential tradeoff is strongly influenced by the level of the discount rate. The lower the discount rate, the greater the willingness to invest in projects with prospects of long-term growth.

Policies that affect discount rates have clear impact on the intertemporal allocation of investment and, by extension, on future productivity and competitiveness. Lower discount rates, especially relative to other nations that are competing for global resources, attract capital in greater amounts. In addition, lower discount rates prejudice investors toward projects where nearer term returns are sacrificed in favor of longer term growth and advantage.

To restate the point, where discount rates are lower investors will favor long-term growth over current profits. As interest rates rise investors will shift their preferences away from growth and toward shorter term profitability.

At a time when investments represent a relatively permanent commitment of infrastructure, investors' orientation to the future is a key determinant of relative national competitive positions in the future. Countries whose policies lead to lower discount rates, which promote investments promising longer term growth, are more likely to dominate the competitive environment in the future. Countries where high discount rates bias investors against the longer term and toward the shorter term will be more advantaged in the near term, but will suffer loss of competitiveness and relative economic viability in the future.

Capital Controls and Discount Rates

Diversification and Discount Rates

In a liberal capital market, discount rates are set by investors as the rate of return they require for investment in a particular project. This rate is set in comparison with other investment alternatives and required returns are determined as compensation for the relative risks incurred in each project. Projected investment returns must exceed the hurdle or threshold rate that would compensate the investor for the diversion of funds from his/her next best investment. Investors must be persuaded that a particular project will provide returns that exceed a real and risk-free rate of interest by increments that are sufficient to compensate for expected inflation and additional risk. That is, investors shift away from growth projects as inflation and risk increase and the required rate of return rises. For example, when interest rates rise investors either look for projects with shorter term returns or demand increasingly higher rates of expected growth to offset the higher discounting on future returns.

Modern financial theory, especially modern portfolio theory, offers us important insights into the relationship between increases in risk and increases in investors' required returns. It is the essence of these theories and perspectives that present a major challenge to those who would include capital controls as an element of growth policy.

Portfolio theory demonstrates that required returns and discount rates, as perceived by an investor, are substantially diminished when opportunities for diversification are available. In Chapter 4, Richard Sweeney presents the basic portfolio model and shows that this model allows investors and managers to "price" various risks and thereby greatly improve their evaluation of projects. He shows that this ability to "free ride" on the pricing qualities of global markets is a significant advantage to decision makers. He argues that significant welfare losses are incurred if capital controls prevent efficient and adequate assessment of investment and operating possibilities in the emerging economies.

In this chapter we build on this perspective and consider the effect of capital controls on the level of discount rates and, consequently, on the attraction and intertemporal allocations of investment funds.

Investors assess the level of risk of a project and incorporate this assessment in the discount rate they apply to that project. Modern portfolio theory's contribution teaches that this assessment is made in the context of the projects' *marginal addition to the risk of investors' existing portfolios.* Further, the marginal addition of risk is less where potential investment projects are considered for addition to portfolios whose risks are reasonably uncorrelated with the risks of this project. The less the correlation between the risks of the prospective project and the risk of the existing portfolio, the less the marginal additional risk of the new project. Further, the prospective project's risks are less likely to be correlated with the current portfolio profile, the larger and more diverse is that investment profile. For instance, the risk of a project in isolation is often reduced by as much as 70–80 percent when that project is added to a portfolio of as few as 20 to 30 randomly selected securities.[10]

As with investments in financial securities, the diversification potential of an investment is often the most important determinant of that investment's discount rate. When opportunities for diversification are very high, the discount rate applied by the investor is significantly reduced. As demonstrated above, this reduction favors investment in longer term growth opportunities.

Capital Controls and Investor Diversification

When capital controls effectively segment local from global capital markets, *the ability of investors to diversify their risk may be severely limited.* Effective capital controls eliminate investors' abilities to tap the diversification potential that is inherent in any project where the controls apply. When opportunities for diversificationare foreclosed, higher rates are applied to investments in infrastructure and reconstruction.

By increasing the discount rate applied to investment projects, capital controls clearly retard the flow of investment resources. However, the additional impact of capital controls on intertemporal resource allocation may be even more destructive and pervasive because the reduction in investment activity will be most intense among projects that promise higher growth. At a time when emerging countries are competing to build the basic structures of their productive and competitive systems, policies that discourage investor orientation to growth and longer term returns are clearly inconsistent with fundamental development objectives.

Capital Control Bias: Local Investor Versus Foreign Investors

One argument for the imposition of capital controls is that they prevent the release of domestic capital resources that would otherwise "flee" to more attractive projects outside the country. Rather than lose domestic capital, the controls attempt to force application of local capital resources to local investment opportunities. Without capital controls, it is reasoned, local investment projects would be forced to compete for funding with projects abroad. The effect would be to raise the costs of capital to local investments and, in consequence, reduce the development of the local economy as fewer local investment options are exercised.

This logic neglects the effects of capital controls on the investors' range of choices and, particularly, on the degree of diversification potential that the investor enjoys. In addition, the traditional argument also ignores the differential effect of capital controls on local investors as opposed to global or foreign investors.

In practice, capital controls are more likely to reduce possibilities for diversification for local investors than they are for foreign investors. By restricting local investors' abilities to expand their portfolios into global markets, capital controls raise the cost of achieving the maximum diversification advantage. Foreign or global investors, on the other hand, suffer no similar restriction. Foreign investors' assessment of a discount rate assumes full diversification advantage because it is incremental to a globally diversified portfolio. As demonstrated above, this advantage confirms a *lower effective discount rate* on global investors relative to local investors. The discount rate advantage will be largest for projects with significant diversification potential.

The discount rate advantage also depends on the extent to which the local economy is linked through trade and other channels to the global economy. If the linkage is tight and the local and global economies respond in concert to economic shocks, there will be little inherent advantage to diversifying outside of the country. Local investors can get close to complete diversification with internal investments. However, if the country relies on a small number of products for economic viability, the diversification advantage is large. In the case where large shocks are experienced differently locally from globally, significant advantage to diversifying outside the country may exist. In this case, local investors are at a large disadvantage if diversification opportunities are denied them.

For any given investment possibility, the global investor will place a higher value on growth and future returns than will local investors. The global investor will outbid local investors for most projects, particularly those that promise high growth.

These dynamics will push local investors, who must earn a higher rate of return since they are not able to diversify their risks, toward projects that are riskier and offer short-term payoffs rather than growth. It is worth noting that local investors seeking higher returns will necessarily orient toward projects that offer higher returns by virtue of greater risk. Local investors will tend to bid competitively on projects that have high overall risk and will generally be successful in bidding on projects that have high risk and low diversification potential. This means that local investors will bear a relatively high share of unsystematic risk. Investments that are less sensitive to swings in the overall market place, but highly sensitive to specific risks, will be relatively attractive to foreign investors. Local investors will be on a more level playing field with regard to the acquisition of highly cyclical investments, especially those with little specific risk and will not be routinely outbid on such projects.

Capital Controls and Economic Prosperity

Investment Analysis and Modern Portfolio Theory

As shown by the analysis above, capital controls may have the effect of raising the discount rate to all investors and will certainly raise rates for domestic investors above those available to global investors.[11] The rate differential will be caused by controls that eliminate the opportunity for domestic investors to diversify their risk. To the extent that these controls are not applied to, or are less effective for, global investors, a discount rate disadvantage will occur. The greater the diversification potential that is denied to domestic investors, the greater the size of the rate disadvantage.

Further, the game is played out against a background of a large number of emerging countries, each realizing the importance of attracting and allocating capital efficiently. Investment opportunities in nations that eschew controls are assessed as being more valuable than those in countries that impose controls. Thus, at a time when the emerging countries are attracting investment to build infrastructure and to develop modern industrial economies, capital will flow first to countries where value is highest and constraints on capital flows are lowest. The attraction will not only be for global investors, but also for local investors. To the extent that controls are effective, local investors will have less incentive to invest locally and will respond to a large incentive to invest abroad. In fact, the strongest pull for local investment funds will be neighboring countries where investor proximity insures greater ability to monitor and control. Thus, capital controls will encourage local capital resources to flow to direct competitors for investment funds and also for industrial business.

This consideration may be especially important in the competition between smaller countries in the same geographic region. Such countries may already be in competition for funds from investors that are drawn to the region for advantages shared by all countries. In this case, capital controls will tip a large number of investment decisions away from the controlling country and the opportunity to take advantage of resources and endowments may be lost. Further, countries that are small and close geographically may also have ties of history and culture. In this case, funds from local investors as well as foreign investors may be transferred easily from the country with controls and higher interest rates to the neighboring, uncontrolled country.

In sum, capital controls put domestic investors at a disadvantage relative to global investors. They also put local industry at a disadvantage to industry from other emerging countries.

Capital Controls and Industrial Structure

Classical trade and production theory assumes that the endowments and proportions of capital and labor in a country are the bases for national comparative advantage. These endowments and their application determine the industrial structure of a country, conferring, for example, a competitive advantage on firms in the service industry that locate in a relatively labor-rich country. Likewise, heavy manufacturing is favored in a country that is capital intensive or where capital is in greater supply. In this case, low population levels or low population density would not be a national disadvantage. In the longer term, labor migration may offset initial differences, but the capital-labor ratio, especially at the onset of economic restructuring activities, will certainly influence the direction of industrial development.

If capital controls render a country less capital intensive, or more labor intensive than it would otherwise be, they also will tend to deter investment in industries that require capital intensity. A lower relative investment in basic infrastructure is probably the most detrimental result. With higher discount rates, the future returns provided by investments in airports, roads, and telecommunications systems will be less valuable than with lower discount rates. Investments in education, another "capital investment" that provides returns over the longer term, will be less attractive to private investors than will be educational investments in other countries. Finally, investment in any kind of system that requires front-end expense will tend to be placed in countries without capital controls.

Investment in information technology and the design of organizational structure usually go hand-in-hand with workforce education and training. Further, it is well known that our global system is moving rapidly toward an "information-based" society with rewards going to "knowledge workers." These individuals need not only national infrastructure in information technology and education, but also complementary and enhancing private investment in this basic "human capital" formation. Without such investment, or with investment lower in these areas than it is for competing emerging nations, countries will find themselves uncompetitive in industries that require skilled employees and the use of information and organizational systems.

As we expand our understanding of "capital investment" beyond the traditional definition of machinery and into areas of information, knowledge and other "human capital," we see that the implications of capital controls for industrial development and future national competitiveness are deep and pervasive. Not only will controlled nations find themselves uncompetitive in such traditional industries for intermediate stages of economic development as automobile and steel manufacture, but also in more advanced industries that support a high standard of living. These nations will find their industries and companies falling farther and farther behind as investment in information and education becomes the currency of the future.

Capital Controls: Industrial Ownership, Management and Control

A recent study of relative national productivity by the McKinsie Global Institute shows that the high standard of living enjoyed in the United States is due, in no small part, to U.S. managers' efficient use of real and financial capital to meet customer preferences.[12] The innumerable individual investment and operating decisions that support this efficient application of assets are strongly biased, as shown above, by the discount rate. Countries that tolerate artificially high discount rates as a cost for keeping capital in the country will force managers, owners, and workers to take the shorter term, risk averse perspective, rather than longer term perspective. Throughout the national economy, all individuals, owners and employees alike, will make choices that differ in kind and degree from their competitors abroad. For example, to the extent that global investors are evaluating projects and transacting based on common, global discount rates, their selection and decisions will reflect the other economic realities such as real costs of labor, land, technology and other factors. Local investors will have over-purchased factors that are consumed and reflected as expenses and under-purchased factors, such as technology, that embody an initial investment in exchange for longer term savings.

As shown above, this effect will be strongest among national or local investors for whom diversification opportunities are foreclosed. Local owners and managers, as well as local employees will consistently choose lower investment and lower initial spending and opt for initial payback rather than growth. Because global managers and investors will outbid locals for projects and investment goods that have high diversification potential, locals will be left with investments that are highly cyclical in nature, as well as having lower growth prospects.

Thus, capital controls will affect, indirectly but strongly, ownership and control structures of industry. Local investors will tend to own firms with relatively little investment in capital and technology and without prospects for competitiveness in the industries of the future. Local investors, owners, and managers will be in control of industries that rely on high use of low-skilled labor. One thinks of industries such as garment manufacture and low-level assembly operations.

In stark contrast, industries or companies owned by foreigners are more likely to be globally competitive. Foreign investors will tend to own, control and manage companies that have relatively larger amounts of more modern capital and employ individuals from the emerging middle class and professional classes than will firms owned by local investors. Foreign-owned firms will be influenced by basic economics to continue investment in employee education and training and in the technology needed for future competitiveness.

In sum, by biasing the decisions of local investors, managers and employees toward the shorter term, and by conferring on foreign investors an advantage in the purchase of lower risk and higher growth investments, capital controls do deep, long-term and perhaps even permanent damage to the national structure of ownership and control.

Capital Controls: National Resource Endowment, Population Migration, and International Comparative Advantage

The sections above describe the long-term, pervasive and destructive effects of capital controls on patterns of investment in national industry and infrastructure and on patterns of local versus foreign ownership and control. However, as shown by Sowell (1996) and others, we can increasingly expect population migration to mitigate differences in underlying advantage and, in an abstract sense, to level out the capital/labor proportions across countries.[13] That is, traditional trade and development theory tells us that population will migrate from areas of labor abundance and unemployment to labor scarcity.[14]

With this tendency in mind, let us review the industrial orientation of countries that select capital controls as tools of economic policy. Investment will be relatively focused in cyclical industries that are more labor and less capital intensive and that employ less-skilled workers. To the extent that this characterization differs from the initial resource endowment balance of the country, population will tend to migrate. In countries that have relatively low population and population density, capital controls will encourage the migration of population from abroad to take up employment in the lower skilled jobs. Countries that are inherently "labor intensive" and have large and concentrated populations will provide jobs with low skill requirements, few educational and training opportunities, and low levels of compensation, and will experience labor immigration.

Not only will low-skilled and poorly educated workers migrate in search of positions, but more highly educated persons will also migrate. They will move toward employment in companies that promise future education, opportunity, and higher compensation. To the extent that capital controls force these kinds of companies from the country, or cause them to be owned by foreigners, the more talented and educated members of the population will either migrate abroad or will seek employment in foreign-owned and managed firms at home.

Again, the indirect but pervasive effects of capital controls on population migration are negative and can be substantial.

Capital Controls: Summary and Political Implications

By raising discount rates, in general, and by creating a disadvantage for local relative to global investors, capital controls have a number of significant and detrimental effects. All of the effects are relative; that is, the investment patterns will be worse than they would be without controls and will compare unfavorably to patterns in countries without controls. A summary of the overall effects follows:

- Less investment locally in companies and projects that depend on a large capital base, on technology, and on highly skilled and educated employees
- Less investment in industries that have low cyclical risk and high growth potential
- Less investment in education and infrastructure
- More investment in industries that require and attract less skilled and educated employees and offer lower employee compensation
- Tendency for countries with an inherent labor shortage to attract population migration from abroad in areas of low skill, education, and compensation
- Tendency to lose ambitious and educated local population to employment in growth-oriented and high-technology industries abroad
- National productivity and efficiency decline over time as less investment is applied to real and human capital investments than is applied in competing countries

Controls will bias the structure of ownership and control such that local investors, managers and employees will be a significant disadvantage to foreign investors in the following ways:

- Employment at jobs with lower compensation and less opportunity for training and development

- Ownership and management of companies that get less competitive over time, as their "short-term" orientation brings them sooner to the "mature" phase of an industry and company life cycle
- Less ownership of and investment in newer technologies and activities that are the future of the global economy
- Employment opportunities with higher compensation and greater potential for growth will be in firms that are owned and managed by foreigners.

The political implications of these biases are clear. Only the severity, extent and consequences of discontent is in question.

In recent times, we have seen strong evidence that national polity is increasingly aware of conditions of prosperity and personal freedom in other countries, especially countries deemed to be "in competition." The polity is more likely to regard as competitors countries that are closer geographically and more alike in terms of basic resources, history and culture. It is increasingly likely that national governments will be held responsible for policies that obstruct their citizens in their search for prosperity and personal freedom, especially if the conditions and results in "competing" countries are more successful.

Forecasts of specific political responses to the conditions listed above require use of models of political economy and public choice. The important contributions of the analysis presented here are that national opportunities for prosperity, growth, and competitiveness will be compromised by the imposition of capital controls. Coming at a time when basic structures and patterns are being established, these impediments will not be easily reversed. Further, ownership patterns and operating choices within the countries will reflect a seeming preference for foreigners and disadvantage for nationals that will seem to arise from both the private enterprise system in general and from public policy choices in particular. It is not too great a stretch to imagine the impact on national perceptions of fairness in a democratic system.

Notes

I am grateful to Dick Sweeney and Tom Willett for helpful discussions. These ideas were initially presented at conferences sponsored by Georgetown University and Tallinn Technical University and discussion at these meetings was helpful. Any errors remain my own.

1. Guitián, Chapter 2, p. 20, this volume.
2. For a cogent discussion of the role of institutional factors in national growth, prosperity and comparative advantage, see Olson (1996).
3. Sweeney, Chapter 4, pp. 47–49, this volume.
4. This valuation formulation assumes a discount rate, *COC*, that is constant across periods.

5. This formulation and its derivation is described in Brealey and Myers (1991: 40–41). Also see Chapter 6 in Weston *et al.* (1990). An additional reference regarding the application of valuation models can be found in Higgins (1995: 278–325). In addition to the assumption of constant growth, the abstraction requires a large number of time intervals and that the growth rate be less than the rate applied as the cost of capital.

6. From the policy perspective, this implies that investment resources can arise from either foreign or domestic sources. Domestic savings, which may have previously fled the country might be returned home, or new savings stimulated from within, if the investment value is sufficiently attractive.

7. Olson (1996).

8. This tendency to shift investor preference away from growth projects as discount rates increase is fundamentally exponential in form. That is, as rates rise the attractiveness of longer term growth projects falls at increasingly rapid rates.

9. Investment in labor-enhancing capital is used here as an example. However, the model can, of course, be very generally applied to any opportunity to replace variable and ongoing costs with a fixed, up-front investment. Energy-saving investments are another familiar class of examples.

10. For a more complete and very accessible discussion of the effects of diversification on risk, see Fruhan *et al.* (1992: 407–20).

11. See Ross (1976), Lessard (1976), and Solnick (1974, 1988).

12. *Capital Productivity*, McKinsie Global Institute, 1996. Referenced in Lewis, "The Wealth of a Nation," *Wall Street Journal*, June 7, 1996.

13. Sowell (1996).

14. Influential nationals in the former Soviet republics were aware of this force of migration during the Communist era. Those in charge of national planning in the relatively labor-scare republics soon realized that to accept investment from Russia in large levels of manufacturing capital meant, not only damage to the environment, but also supporting influxes of Russian workers to take up excess employment opportunities. For nationalistic reasons, some of these planners avoided making their countries appear too attractive as sites for substantial capital investment from Russia.

References

Brealey, Richard A. and Stewart C. Myers. 1991. *Principles of Corporate Finance*, 4th ed. New York: McGraw-Hill, Inc.

Bower, Dorothy H., Richard S. Bower and Dennis E. Logue. 1987. "A Primer on Arbitrage Pricing Theory," in Joel M. Stern and Donald H. Chew, Jr., eds., *The Revolution in Corporate Finance.* Pp. 69–77. New York: Basil Blackwell.

Fruhan, William E., *et al.* 1992. "Diversification, the Capital Asset Pricing Model, and the Cost of Equity Capital," in *Case Problems in Finance,* 10th ed. Pp. 407–20. Boston: Irwin.

Guitián, Manuel. 1996. "Reality and the Logic of Capital Flow Liberalization," in Christine Ries and Richard Sweeney, eds., *Capital Controls in Emerging Economies*. Pp. 17–32. Boulder, Colo.: Westview Press.

Higgins, Robert C. 1995. *Analysis for Financial Management*, 4th ed. Boston: Irwin.

Lessard, Donald R. 1976. "World, Country and Industry Relationship in Equity Returns: Implications for Risk Reduction Through International Diversification." *Financial Analysts Journal*, January-February: 32–38.

Lewis, Bill. 1996. "The Wealth of a Nation." *Wall Street Journal,* June 7, Sec. A, p. 12.

McKinsie Global Institute. 1996. *Capital Productivity*. Washington D.C., June.

Olson, Mancur. 1996. "Big Bills Left on the Sidewalk: Why Some Nations Are Rich, and Others Are Poor." *Journal of Economic Perspectives* 10(2): 3–24.

Ross, Stephen A. 1976. "The Arbitrage Theory of Capital Asset Pricing." *Journal of Economic Theory* 13: 31–60.

Shapiro, Alan C. 1991. *Foundations of Multinational Financial Management*. Chapter 16, pp. 365–80 and Chapter 18, pp. 408–41. Boston: Allyn and Bacon.

Solnick, Bruno. 1974. "Why Not Diversify Internationally Rather Than Domestically?" *Financial Analysts Journal*, July-August: 48–54.

———. 1988. *International Investments.* Reading, Mass.: Addison-Wesley.

Sowell, Thomas. 1996. *Migration and Cultures: A World View*. New York: Basic Books.

Sweeney, Richard J. 1997. "The Information Costs of Capital Controls," in Christine Ries and Richard Sweeney, eds., *Capital Controls in Emerging Economies*. Pp. 45–61. Boulder, Colo.: Westview Press.

Weston, J. Fred, Kwang S. Chung, and Susan E. Hoag. 1990. *Mergers, Restructuring and Corporate Control.* Chapter 6, pp. 132–63. Englewood Cliffs, N.J.: Prentice Hall.

7

Capital Account Liberalization and Policy Incentives: An Endogenous Policy View

Clas Wihlborg and Thomas D. Willett

Introduction

Advocates of restrictions on international capital mobility tend to view capital flows as a frequently destabilizing exogenous element that complicates the task of economic policymaking. Modern monetary and financial analysis, however, stresses that the effects of changes in economic variables such as interest rates, exchange rates and capital flows depend critically on the underlying causes of the changes. Most commonly, capital flows respond to expectations about underlying economic conditions and policies. Frequently, capital flows viewed as exogenous, destabilizing complications by officials attempting to maintain a pegged exchange rate in fact represent rational, endogenous responses to economic policy developments: they are messengers signaling that there are serious concerns about the stability of domestic economic policies. Not surprisingly, these two views have profoundly different implications for policy.

The first view, that capital flows are typically exogenous destabilizing factors, suggests the need for heavy regulation of financial flows. The second, that capital flows are largely rational, endogenous responses to underlying conditions, suggests that policies, rather than market responses, are disruptive. It is not surprising that policy officials tend to incline toward the first view. We argue that the evidence suggests that the explanatory power of the second view is greater, although identification of the fundamental cause of capital flows in a particular time and place is always uncertain.

The distinction between exogenous and endogenous factors also suggests an important role that international capital flows can play in helping to generate more stable and efficiency-increasingeconomic policies. Traditionally, economists studied the effects of exogenous changes in economic policies. In recent years, developments in both public choice and macroeconomic analysis have pointed to the importance of endogenizing policy in our analysis. Macroanalysis has emphasized that the effects of policy changes may vary tremendously depending on whether the changes are anticipated or not; public choice analysis has emphasized factors that influence the incentives for government decision makers to adopt stable and efficiency-increasing policies. Typically, higher international capital mobility increases the costs of unstable and efficiency-decreasing domestic policies; thus, if one takes the course of policies as given, i.e., exogenous, there is a plausible second-best argument that restricting capital mobility is desirable to minimize the costs of specific policies. This view underlies the frequently expressed proposition that the creation of domestic macroeconomic stability is a necessary precondition for establishing capital account convertibility, i.e., allowing freedom of capital flows.

Endogenous policy theory turns this argument on its head. For the very reason that free capital movements increase the costs of certain domestic policies, they create incentives for governments to follow policies that are desirable from an efficiency point of view. From the standpoint of creating institutional structures designed to improve incentives for policymakers to pursue efficiency-increasing policies, there is a seldom recognized similarity between the case for central bank independence and for freedom of capital mobility.

The next section discusses the implications of our view of endogenous policy for the relation between capital account convertibility and monetary discipline. This view has implications for the sequencing of liberalization as discussed in the third section. Factors influencing incentives to liberalize capital account transactions are reviewed in the fourth section. Then the interdependence between incentives to liberalize domestic financial markets and capital account transactions is analyzed within the framework of a model presented in the appendix. The final section contains concluding comments.

Speculative Capital Flows and Monetary Discipline

Milton Friedman (1953) argued in his classic re-interpretation of the interwar experience that speculative capital flows, by our standard economic definition, could be stabilizing rather than destabilizing in the sense that they would tend to move the exchange rate toward rather than away from its equilibrium value. Defenders of pegged exchange rates often argued that if speculative capital flows were a problem under pegged rates, they would be much worse under flexible rates; advocates of floating rates countered that it was the emergence of disequilibrium under pegged rates that was the basic cause of the problem, and that under flexible exchange rates stabilizing speculation would not be disruptive but equilibrating.

The post–Bretton Woods experience with flexible exchange rates has not been kind to the belief that speculation will always be strongly stabilizing under floating rates, but neither has this experience offered much support for those who argue that speculative capital flows are inherently unstable. One frequently hears charges of gross over- or undervaluation of currencies under flexible exchange rates, especially the weak dollar of the late 1970s and the strong dollar of the early and mid-1980s, but there were strong economic reasons for the fall and rise of the dollar.[1] The charge against speculative behavior that must be taken more seriously is that if underlying shocks and policies and plausible expectations of their continuation generate large movements in exchange rates, then speculative dynamics may develop which push currencies too far up or down. Thus, speculative capital flows may exacerbate the disruptive effects of unstable conditions, but they seldom are initiators of disruptive situations.[2]

As noted, the shift to viewing capital flows as endogenous rather than exogenous has been extended to economic policy as well. Traditionally, economic analysis has focused on the effects of changes in economic policy. The development of public choice analysis, which showed that politically optimal economic policies may sometimes be destabilizing, and the rational expectations revolution, which emphasized the difference in effects of anticipated versus unanticipated policy changes, combined to focus the efforts of many economists on endogenous policy.[3] A major strand of this literature focuses on the design of incentive structures or constraint systems that reduce the propensity of policymakers to take destabilizing economic policy actions for short-run political advantages. Such considerations have been at the forefront in discussions of the European Monetary System and proposals for the use of pegged exchange rates to provide nominal anchors for anti-inflation policies in developing countries and the former communist economies.[4]

The comparative effects of pegged versus flexible exchange rates in providing domestic discipline is an open issue. Under either system, international capital mobility provides incentives for disciplined economic policies. In the context of the European Monetary System, this has been explicitly recognized as a major reason for the liberalization of capital flows.[5] The same argument holds for any market economy. The weight given to this consideration increases with the need of governments to establish the credibility of their policies and with the difficulties of making credible commitments in other ways. On both scores, freedom of capital flows seems particularly useful for many developing and former communist countries.

Capital flows tend to have a disciplinary effect on government policy under two conditions. First, speculative capital flows and speculative crises occur primarily as the result of economic policies that generate expectations about future inflation and depreciation. Second, the probability that specific policies will generate speculative capital flows strengthens the incentives for governments to conduct anti-inflationary policies in the first place. Neither of these conditions is uncontroversial. The first condition implies that capital flows are not simply exogenous but that they are the result of (a) a shift to more restrictive policies abroad, (b) less restrictive policies domestically, or (c) reasonable expectations about future shifts in domestic or foreign policies.

Consider first, for example, a shift to more restrictive monetary policies abroad, causing a capital outflow.[6] Then, if capital mobility is high, capital flows induce the monetary authority to follow the lead of the foreign, more-restrictive policy. The alternative is to allow a depreciation. If, on the other hand, domestic authorities are responsible for increased inflationary pressure causing capital outflows, then the result under high capital mobility is either a balance of payments crisis or an exchange rate depreciation and inflation. In this case, the increased responsiveness of capital flows tends to contribute to monetary discipline because inflationary tendencies would show more quickly after a shift towards a more expansionary policy.

As a third case, assume that capital outflows are caused by expectations that future domestic governments will conduct more expansionary policies. If the current government intends to keep its anti-inflationary stance, it must allow long-term interest rates to rise. This effect is strengthened by higher capital mobility. It is costly for the current government to maintain its stance in this situation, assuming that it has to bear the political costs of a higher interest rate. Under these conditions, the anti-inflationary government's incentive to relax its monetary restraint increases with the degree of capital mobility and with the probability that it will be replaced by a more inflationary government.

Another case in which the effects of higher capital mobility may be perverse involves fiscal deficits that are unaccompanied by monetary expansion. Capital inflows reduce the domestic interest-rate effects of a deficit and, hence, may reduce the government's concern about them in the short run. A number of economists have argued that this has been a problem within the EMS, as well as with the U.S. budget deficits in the 1980s.[7]

This reasoning indicates that capital mobility does not always act as a disciplinary device for a government, even if the government's policies are responsive to capital flows. The disciplinary effects of capital outflows are present for a government that is reasonably secure in power, but not always for shaky governments that may be replaced soon by a more inflationary government. Capital mobility is accordingly not a sufficiently strong mechanism to substitute for domestic mechanisms to generate monetary discipline. One such mechanism is central bank independence.

The Sequencing of Liberalization

There has been much debate about the proper sequencing of economic liberalization. Standard analysis suggests, for example, that it is not a good idea to liberalize the capital account before liberalizing domestic financial markets. This need not imply, however, that capital account liberalization should follow domestic financial market liberalization by a substantial period of time. As Woo (1993) has recently argued, most of the sequencing literature is based on the assumption that policymakers can only liberalize one market at a time. It is not clear that in most cases domestic financial market liberalization and opening of the capital account would not optimally occur virtually simultaneously.[8]

Traditionally, capital controls advocates have been primarily concerned with the problem of capital outflows. Since the mid-1980s, however, concerns have also focused on the possibility of "excessive" capital inflows. Economic liberalization and policy reforms could prove to be "too credible." Large net capital inflows could cause substantial appreciation of the real exchange rate, either directly under flexible exchange rates, or by inducing monetary expansion and inflation under a pegged exchange rate. Such real appreciations could in turn substantially reduce prospects for export expansion. The classic example usually cited is Chile.[9] More recently, Mexico is also frequently cited.

In the case of Mexico, many commentators have expressed concern that large capital inflows have primarily taken the form of financial capital flows rather than direct investment flows. Some argue not only that this short-term lending and portfolio investment does not help growth in Mexico, but that such financial inflows also make Mexico much more vulnerable to speculative crisis. There is some evidence that direct investment flows tend to be less variable than other capital account items, and that countries with high ratios of foreign direct investment have been less likely to develop balance of payments crises.[10] Direct investment may also be associated with greater micro benefits for the receiving country in terms of the transfer of technology and skills. Thus, we do not want to argue that direct investment inflows may not be especially desirable. But we are skeptical of the view that other forms of capital inflows cannot help growth. Given the fungibility of different sources of financing, capital inflows need not go straight into direct investment for them to have the effect of increasing domestic investment. The proportion of financial inflows that finance increased domestic investment can be strongly influenced by a country's monetary and fiscal policies. Loose monetary and fiscal policies generate inflation and uncertainty that reduce the incentives to invest. Under such conditions much of any capital inflow would end up financing government expenditures and private consumption. However, with sound monetary and fiscal policies, the incentives for funds to flow into investment would be substantially increased.[11] The incentives of financial institutions are also important for the effective recycling of financial investments from abroad.

We are skeptical of arguments that large financial claims by foreigners due to accumulated capital inflows make a country especially susceptible to speculative crisis. For one reason, seldom would a situation develop in which large outflows of foreign funds would not be accompanied by substantial flight of domestic capital; according to IMF reports, the Mexican peso crisis in the fall of 1994 was triggered by portfolio shifts of Mexican residents. Thus, the greater "exposure" of the country to international capital flows would likely be one of degree, not of kind. For another reason, there are few if any cases where a crisis has been generated by foreign capital outflows in situations where the country is following prudent economic policies.

The issue of the effects of capital inflows on the real exchange rate and hence on the traded goods sector is more complicated. Substantial resource transfers to developing and former communist countries require that they run current account deficits. How this should be balanced with the possible advantages of export-led growth lies well beyond the scope of this paper. We strongly suspect, however, that for some time to come most of the former communist countries will face a problem of having below rather than above optimum levels of new financial inflows, whatever this optimum might be.

As the case of Chile illustrates, however, where there are substantial problems with domestic incentive structures, capital inflows can make the situation worse. For example, if the agents receiving loans from abroad face distorted domestic incentives, then the resulting misallocation of funds could leave the country as a whole poorer. The larger the capital inflows the greater would be this effect. The ideal solution, of course, is to get the domestic incentives right, but this will not always be feasible, especially quickly. Such concerns are, of course, what has given rise to the literature on sequencing.[12] This debate is well founded, but we caution that concern over the possibility of capital flows magnifying the costs of domestic distortions can be taken too far, as in some discussions of the necessary preconditions for currency convertibility. We discuss the economic and political interaction between domestic distortions and capital account liberalization in the next section in the framework of a simple model.

In considering the issue from a practical policy point of view, it is important to distinguish, as not all of the literature has, between conditions under which capital flows, foreign exchange markets, etc. will work best and those conditions under which freeing exchange rates and capital flows and removing trade barriers will improve or worsen the current situation. For example, in their useful summary of the debate about currency convertibility, Greene and Isard (1991) describe the economics literature as having "identified certain preconditions that must prevail if currency convertibility is to be implemented successfully" (p. 9). It is not entirely clear to us from the subsequent discussion what type of meaning to ascribe to "successful implementation" in light of the distinction made above. The statement could easily be taken as suggesting that currency convertibility should not be implemented until a country's economic house was fully in order. One of the four "basic requirements" listed is "an environment in which economic agents have both the incentives and the ability to respond to market prices, from which all major distortions should have been eliminated" (p. 9). We know of no economy that meets this requirement fully, but we doubt that the existence of highly price-distorting agricultural policies in Europe and the United States has any substantial influence on the cases for and against current and capital account convertibility in these countries.

More common are views, as in Hanson (1995), that "the first precondition to international financial liberalization is a stable macroeconomy" (p. 395), but even this conclusion may be too strong. Capital flows will undoubtedly be more stable when the domestic economy is stable, and for a high-inflation country it would certainly be wise to launch a serious stabilization effort before opening the capital account. It is not clear, however, that liberalization should be delayed for the number of years typically needed for a stabilization effort to be completed. As Guitián (1995) has noted, waiting for ideal conditions "to materialize before proceeding to liberalize capital movements may be the best recipe for the permanence of capital controls" (p. 85). Wihlborg and Dezseri also discuss this issue in Chapter 3 above.

What is needed is more detailed analysis of the ways in which the costs of different types of economic policy inefficiencies would likely be influenced by the freedom of capital flows. We conjecture that a general result from such detailed analysis would be that where the domestic inefficiency cannot be corrected directly there would typically be some offsetting policy available that would fall far short of general capital controls. The analogy between efficiency aspects of capital controls and commercial policy in the presence of domestic distortions is discussed in the next section.

In such analysis, it is important to consider not only static effects generated from current distortions but also dynamic effects on the likely evolution of policies over time. Initiation of a policy with given economic effects may stimulate different political dynamics in different countries. The research agenda we suggest is far from easy, but it is one of considerable importance.

Capital Account Convertibility and Liberalization Incentives

The economic arguments for liberalizing current account transactions before capital account transactions depend generally on distortions in goods and factor markets, adjustment costs, the need for macroeconomic stabilization, and domestic financial market distortions. Most arguments rely on assumptions about policy failures or policy-created distortions that make capital account convertibility potentially immiserating.

The arguments over the timing of capital account liberalization are reviewed separately in this volume by Wihlborg and Dezseri (Chapter 3). We can distinguish between arguments against an early liberalization of the capital account on the grounds either of capital inflows or of capital outflows. Edwards and Edwards (1991, 1992), Frenkel (1982, 1983), McKinnon (1991) and others warn that inflows following liberalization may cause a real appreciation and excessive credit expansion. The credit expansion is worsened by a banking system that does not evaluate credit risk properly. Krueger (1984) points to the misallocation caused by capital inflows when domestic investments are based on distorted prices in goods and factor markets. In general, it is distortions in goods, factor or credit markets that render capital inflows undesirable. The distortions are, as noted, taken as given in the analysis of capital account liberalization; the policy implication is that the distortions or the policies causing distortions, such as insurance of the banking system or protection of domestic industries, should be removed before capital account controls are lifted.

Economic problems caused by capital outflows following liberalization were discussed above in connection with issues of monetary stabilization. Another often-cited problem is that net capital outflows reduce the share of domestic savings available for domestic real investment. Such net outflows are not welfare decreasing for the country as a whole, however, unless there are positive externalities associated with the use of domestic savings in the home country or with investment in the home country in excess of the level chosen at prevailing interest rates and returns.

The capital inflow problem would occur when capital account liberalization is part of a larger liberalization package and this package is credible. The outflow problem is associated with a lack of credibility of monetary or market liberalization policies of current or future governments. In most cases, except when a potential future government lacking credibility is the cause of capital outflows, it is at least formally in the power of the current government to remove the market failures or the policies responsible for the negative welfare consequences of capital flows.

The modern theory of economic policy endogenizes government policy by considering the incentives for governments to pursue a set of policy objectives over the short and the long run, and by considering expectations in the private sector about policy behavior. Before turning to an analysis of capital account convertibility within the framework of the modern theory of endogenous policy, we consider political economy arguments relating to the dynamics of economic policies towards market distortions. In particular, Hayek (1960) analyses the consequences of strong distributional policy objectives for the dynamics of regulation of market activity. His argument is that the imposition of, for example, price controls or quantitative restrictions in one market tends to lead to political pressures for increasingly severe restrictions both in the market subject to initial regulation and other related markets. Assume, for example, that policymakers introduce rent controls for egalitarian reasons. Black markets tend to develop; also, property owners may sell apartments instead of renting them, shrinking the stock of apartments subject to rent control. Political pressures for further regulation in the housing market, as well as in the housing-credit market, arise when large groups observe that the purpose of rent control is being defeated by individuals seeking to maximize their wealth.

During the last decade of deregulation Hayek's political dynamics seem to have worked in reverse, with efficiency dominating equity as a policy objective.[13] Deregulation and the relaxation of price controls in one market increase the imbalances and the economic or political costs of restrictions in another market. For example, if credit markets are liberalized, the access to credit for purchases of housing and condominiums improves, for the relatively well off in particular. As a consequence, the housing stock available at controlled rents shrinks. Excess demand in the controlled market increases, and black market transactions expand. The efficiency-seeking public would in this case accept further deregulation.

It is a reasonable hypothesis that neither Hayek's process of increasing restrictions on market transactions nor the process of deregulation goes on without limit. Rather, each country would reach a certain "political equilibrium" characterized by some restrictions on market activities and the acceptance of some evasion of the restrictions through black market activities. The political equilibrium varies across countries depending on voters' valuation of equity versus efficiency and the institutional structures through which they make known their valuations. The model presented below captures this idea.

In industrialized countries like Sweden the deregulation of capital account transactions, as well as the liberalization of domestic financial markets, can be understood in light of the dynamic processes. During the 1950s through the 1970s price and quantitative controls in financial markets played an important role in Sweden in a program intended to increase the supply of low-cost apartments. The credit allocation objective of the government could not be achieved without restrictions on capital flows. In the 1980s, real GDP growth became a more important objective than achieving housing-policy goals by means of credit allocation. At the same time, the savings rate was low and the government's use of financial resources had increased. With new objectives in mind, interest rates were liberalized and quantitative controls on credit allocation removed during the years 1982–85. Foreign exchange restrictions remained in effect, but the costs of enforcing them increased when domestic markets were liberalized. Furthermore, restrictions on borrowing abroad in combination with a low domestic savings rate hindered Swedish firms' investment activities. Government borrowing abroad had been discredited by the foreign debt that was built up in the late 1970s and had received some blame for relaxing the government's budget constraint. In brief, the costs of not allowing freedom of capital flows became obvious after the liberalization of domestic financial markets. Most exchange restrictions were removed during the period 1986–89.[14]

The idea that government-induced distortions or liberalization in one market can cause further distortions or liberalization in other markets through the political process can be applied to the relationship between capital account regulation and regulatory distortions in other markets. The appendix contains a stylized model that highlights the assumptions required for capital account liberalization to contribute to further liberalization in domestic financial markets or goods markets. Protectionist trade policies can be considered examples of goods-market distortions. We also seek determinants of the "politically optimal" liberalization of capital account transactions.

In the model a government can impose regulatory constraints on quantities or prices in domestic financial markets. It may also use taxes or subsidies, but we discuss these policies separately. We define a variable, D, capturing the severity of interventionist policy. This variable could be interpreted as the number of markets in which quantity and/or price regulations are imposed. When policies simply correct for market failures D equals zero, but D increases as policies cause distortions in the markets.

The government's motivation for causing such distortions is that it has policy objectives beyond pure economic efficiency. Distributional objectives are, of course, prominent and often pursued by interventionist policies, though such policies often are not "first-best" policies to achieve distributional objectives. We assume initially that governments cannot use simple tax and transfer policies to achieve these objectives. This assumption is relaxed when tax and subsidy policies are considered below. Real exchange rate objectives could also be important. It is reasonable to assume that there is a real appreciation as markets are liberalized.

The conflict the government faces in the model is that as market intervention expands beyond the point at which market failures are corrected, economic efficiency declines while (1) distributional objectives are achieved to an increasing extent and (2) the real exchange rate depreciates, favoring the exporting sector.

Necessary conditions for an "equilibrium" degree of intervention to exist are that with increases in *D*, efficiency losses increase at an increasing rate (increasing marginal cost) while the government's perception of welfare due to the achievement of distributional and real exchange rate objectives grows at a smaller, constant or declining rate. We believe these assumptions are realistic. Intervention in only one market may affect efficiency to a negligible extent while being useful from a distributional perspective. As intervention expands, efficiency losses mount at an increasing rate as private incentives are allowed to operate without restriction in fewer and fewer markets. At the same time, marginal benefits from achieving more distributional and real exchange rate objectives decline. Without these assumptions, corner solutions result.

Hayek's conclusion that government interventions with distributional objectives tend to lead to a self-perpetuating spiral of regulatory intervention does not generally hold in our framework because there is a level of intervention at which the perceived marginal benefits equal the marginal costs, and the change in net marginal benefits from an increase in intervention is negative. This conclusion depends on the assumptions about the perceived marginal costs and benefits of interventionary policies.

The government in our model can also insure households, firms and financial institutions against risk; the variable capturing the degree of insurance of the private sector is called *G*. This variable equals zero at a level where it only corrects market failures such as a possibility of a run on the banking system. As the insurance coverage increases, there are efficiency losses due to activities characterized by moral hazard; these considerations are particularly important in the financial sector. Efficiency losses rise at an increasing rate with *G*. The benefits of insurance are consumer protection and perceived benefits of reduced risk. These benefits increase at a lower rate than efficiency losses. Thus, if insurance coverage is considered in isolation, there is a political-economy "equilibrium" level above zero.

Direct intervention in markets and insurance interact as well. We assume that economic efficiency losses from intervention (*D*) and insurance (*G*) depend on an interactive term. In financial markets, for example, restrictions on asset choice could be used by regulators to reduce risk-taking that is deemed excessive because of insurance of financial market participants. It is assumed that the interactive term has a positive effect on economic efficiency although it is possible to envision other outcomes. A more detailed specification of relevant markets is required to analyze how efficiency is influenced by a combination of insurance and direct intervention, but we consider our assumption realistic for many types of regulatory measures, when these are implemented to offset the distorting effects of insurance policies.

Finally, we introduce the degree of capital account convertibility. Like intervention in domestic financial markets, capital account restrictions affect both efficiency and distributional objectives. In the model in the appendix, we are primarily concerned with the effects of capital account convertibility on efficiency costs and benefits of domestic regulatory policies to achieve egalitarian and insurance objectives. In addition, we assume that for a certain level of distortions, *D*, with given distributional consequences, increased convertibility causes an increase in the efficiency losses of domestic quantitative and price restrictions captured by *D*. Similarly, for a certain level of insurance offered to financial market participants, the efficiency losses caused by moral hazard increase with capital account convertibility. The richer menu of financial assets available with convertibility raises enforcement costs for achieving the domestic policy objectives.

The model also incorporates intertemporal aspects of the government's policy preferences. These aspects are interesting because the costs in terms of economic efficiency from distortions tend to appear after some time, but distributional and insurance objectives are achieved rapidly.[15] Regulatory intervention may also decrease in effectiveness over time with respect to distributional objectives; we do not specifically model this latter aspect, which is captured qualitatively by the relative increase over time in the weight of the efficiency loss.

Intertemporal aspects are also important because current policy preferences are influenced by expectations about future government policies. The results below are based on the simple assumption that the government and the private sector have identical expectations and they are such that any current policy shift is expected to be permanent. The permanence assumption is obviously not realistic, but an increase in the discount rate with expectations about permanent shifts has the same effect on the equilibrium as expectations about, for example, reversals of policy in the future.

Financial Market Liberalization and Convertibility

In this section we present a brief summary and intuitive explanations of the main conclusions derived from the model presented above. The initial assumption is that the government uses interventionist policies to achieve distributional objectives; tax and subsidy policies are considered thereafter. In other words, "first-best" policies cannot be used. Under the stated assumptions, the following results are derived in the appendix:

RESULT 1. *Liberalization of the capital account induces liberalization of financial markets (equilibrium D falls) at a constant level of insurance (G) of market participants.*

RESULT 2. *Liberalization of the capital account induces the liberalization of financial markets and a reduction in the equilibrium level of insurance when both these regulatory policy measures are variable and endogenous (equilibrium D and G fall).*[16]

The intuition behind these two results is that the efficiency losses associated with achieving certain levels of distributional and insurance objectives increase with capital account liberalization. Thus, capital account liberalization enhances the credibility of a domestic liberalization program.

RESULT 3. *As the time-horizon of the government is shortened and the likelihood that it will be replaced by a more interventionist government is increased, the equilibrium levels of distortions and insurance increase.*

The most interesting aspect of this result is that a liberalization-oriented government may feel obliged to liberalize less if there is a substantial probability that it will be replaced by a less liberal government. But,

RESULT 4. *Capital account liberalization reduces the reluctance of a short-horizon government to liberalize financial markets.*

Results 3 and 4 depend very much on the assumption about lagged efficiency costs of distortions. The weight of these costs in the government's valuation is reduced when the discount rate rises. Increased capital account convertibility, on the other hand, increases the weight of these costs.

We turn next to endogenous capital account convertibility, as well as endogenous domestic distortions and insurance.

RESULT 5. *If there are efficiency gains from capital account convertibility independent of the levels of distortions and insurance, then there is an equilibrium degree of convertibility from the government's point of view.*

If it is assumed, as in the formal model in the appendix, that efficiency gains of convertibility are interactive with distortions and insurance, but that convertibility *per se* does not increase efficiency, then the government has the incentive to restrict capital mobility severely. This result depends on the relatively large efficiency costs of distortion and insurance which must be incurred to reach specific distributional, real exchange rate, and insurance objectives when capital mobility is high. Realistically, there are efficiency gains from convertibility independent of the levels of distortion and insurance. Therefore the government faces a trade-off between these gains and the costs mentioned above. By analogy to the results presented above, but without proof in the appendix, the following conclusions can be drawn:

RESULT 6. *Exogenous liberalization of financial markets (a reduction in D), and a reduction in the insurance coverage (a reduction in G) induce a higher degree of capital account convertibility.*

This conclusion follows because when, for example, distortions decline, the efficiency losses of using capital account convertibility to achieve distributional objectives increase. Another way of stating this is that when domestic markets are liberalized, capital account restrictions become less effective with respect to egalitarian and insurance objectives.

The important aspect of this result in combination with 2 above is that the different kinds of liberalization are mutually reinforcing. It follows also that:

RESULT 7. *An increase in the discount rate due, for example, to a shorter government time-horizon leads both to a lesser degree of domestic market liberalization and to lesser capital account liberalization under the assumption that all efficiency gains are realized with a lag.*

We noted in our discussion of monetary issues that monetary discipline could be reduced by the prospect of a more inflationary government coming to power when capital mobility is high. The results in 7 are similar. Because an increase in the probability that a government will be voted out of office leads to an increase in the government's discount rate, the incentives to liberalize are reduced. Result 3 above is similar.

We also consider in the appendix that distributional objectives can be achieved by taxes and subsidies. For example, the government can offer an interest rate subsidy on lending for specific purposes. Most of the results hold if *D* is interpreted as taxes and subsidies rather than quantitative restrictions or price controls. One important difference is that the efficiency costs of achieving specific objectives under capital account convertibility are reduced. The lower efficiency costs of achieving distributional objectives have the following implication under the assumption that the government has a preference for direct controls to achieve non-efficiency objectives:

RESULT 8. *Capital account convertibility strengthens the incentive to use taxes and subsidies as opposed to direct market restrictions to achieve distributional objectives.*

Most of the discussion above has been based on the assumption that "first-best" policies to achieve distributional objectives are not available or are considered politically inferior. Distributional objectives are typically achieved at least cost in terms of economic efficiency by direct taxes or transfers to individuals. The efficiency of these measures with respect to distributional objectives can be considered independent of convertibility, and the motivation for market intervention (D) to achieve distributional objectives disappears. Then, the only remaining reason for the government to restrict convertibility and to intervene in domestic financial markets is to offset excessive incentives to accept risk when government insurance exists.

Finally, we ask to what extent can the model be applied to goods markets and current account liberalization. We may interpret D above as the strength of distorting protectionist policies in goods markets and G as government guarantees offered shareholders in domestic firms. As in financial markets, assume that capital account convertibility increases the costs of domestic distortions in goods markets. This argument is used by proponents of delayed convertibility in favor of their cause. In our framework this assumption is important for the result that liberalization of different types is mutually reinforcing. Specifically, the results 2 and 7 above can be applied to the liberalization of the current and capital accounts of the balance of payments respectively. It can be expected that these types of liberalization are mutually reinforcing like domestic financial market and capital account liberalization above.

The general implication we draw from this analysis with respect to sequencing is that liberalization should begin where the political costs of liberalizing are relatively low.

Concluding Remarks

Where does the analysis in this paper leave us with respect to policy recommendations for countries involved in stabilization and liberalization programs? Our strongest conclusion is a negative one: The rationale for the widely received proposition that capital account convertibility should come relatively late in the liberalization process is substantially weakened when endogenous capital-flow and economic policy considerations are taken into account. There are certainly risks to early capital account liberalization, but as is pointed to throughout this volume, there may also be substantial costs to continuing capital controls. We give substantial weight to the argument that a government's willingness to liberalize the capital account gives a substantial boost to the credibility of its reform efforts.

Given all of the recent analysis of the importance of credibility for reducing the costs and increasing the odds of the sustainability of both macro- and microeconomic reform efforts, we are inclined to give considerable weight to the prospect of such potential credibility gains. Our argument presumes, of course, that the reluctance to liberalize depends on fears about the transition process rather than on a reluctance to accept the final result of a liberalization program.

Opponents of "liberalization now" are often opponents of "liberalization at all," however. They may hope that a protracted transition will limit or reverse liberalization in the end. The mutually reinforcing nature of different types of liberalization implies that strong opposition to one kind of liberalization as it arises may be worthwhile as a strategy for slowing down liberalization in general.

The finding that the incentives for capital account and domestic financial liberalization are likely to be mutually reinforcing is encouraging, however. This supports the case for simultaneous early liberalization on both the domestic and international sides; where both cannot be pursued at once, perhaps because of domestic political constraints, movement in one dimension aids the case for subsequent liberalization in the other.

A final point concerns the importance of taking political economy considerations into account in formulating liberalization strategies. Even when optimal sequencing patterns can be identified in terms of economic efficiency criteria, reformers also need to consider the factors that influence the political feasibility of initiating and sustaining reform efforts. Unfortunately, hard research on such issues is in its infancy. Until strong evidence is found to the contrary, we believe that reformers should take advantage of political windows of opportunity as they arise and push for both domestic financial market and capital account liberalization to be initiated as quickly as possible.

Appendix: Modeling Endogenous Financial Market Liberalization and Capital Account Convertibility

The government is assumed to perceive social welfare in period t, w_t, as a function of the degree of distortion in domestic financial markets, D, and the degree of insurance provided investors in financial instruments, G.

Welfare is measured as the deviation from the level achieved when there are no distortions at $D = 0$ and no insurance at $G = 0$:

$$w_t = a_1 D_{t-1}^2 + a_2 G_{t-1}^2 + a_3 D_{t-1} G_{t-1} + a_4 D_t + a_5 G_t. \tag{A1}$$

The present value of these measures of welfare over future periods is

$$P_t(w) = \sum_{j=0}^{\infty} w_{t+j} / (1+r)^j \tag{A2}$$

where $a_1 < 0$, $a_2 < 0$, $a_3 \gtrless 0$, $a_4 > 0$, $a_5 > 0$.

The D-variable can be thought of as interest rate ceilings and quantitative restrictions on the allocation of financial resources. It is the case that $D = 0$ when the government intervenes in the markets only to compensate for market failures; D increases as the number of financial markets subject to some restriction increases and as the degree of restriction in any one market strengthens.

As D increases, distortions reduce economic efficiency with a lag, because the costs of keeping the policy effective with respect to distributional objectives increase as individuals and firms learn to avoid the restrictions. The lagged (squared) values of D in (A1) capture that the efficiency loss increases with D at an increasing rate, as described by the negative parameter a_1 on the squared value of D.

The positive effects of government intervention arise as a result of distributional policy objectives being achieved. Welfare is increasing linearly in D at a rate a_4 as distributional objectives are achieved to an increasing extent.

Government guarantees offered to savers are captured by the term G, as noted. When these guarantees do not simply correct for market failures, economic efficiency losses occur at an increasing rate as the coverage of the guarantees expands. Thus, the parameter $a_2 < 0$. These losses occur with a lag as well. The social benefits of the guarantees are related to, for example, consumer protection, which can be seen as a policy objective. The parameter a_5 is positive and welfare increases linearly as the coverage of guarantees expands.

The interactive term in (A1) with the coefficient a_3 captures, for example, that there are efficiency gains from distortionary policies when there is a level of insurance already in place. For example, if banks' liabilities are insured by the government, a moral hazard problem arises that can be alleviated by government intervention. In the case when regulation reduces a moral hazard problem caused by the government insurance, then $a_3 > 0$. It is possible to envision cases when $a_3 < 0$ as well, but assume for now that $a_3 > 0$.

Capital account convertibility can be captured in two ways in the model. First, the effects of liberalization of capital account transactions are captured by the a-parameters. Relaxation of capital account regulation is just one aspect of capital mobility, and it can be assumed that the degree of capital mobility, defined as the responsiveness of capital flows to risk-adjusted return differentials, influences the a-parameters. Second, capital account restrictions may have independent efficiency and distributional consequences in the same way distortions in domestic markets, captured by D, have such effects. We do not introduce the latter consequences of capital account regulation formally in order to simplify our focus on the interaction between convertibility and distortions in domestic markets.

Optimal levels of D and G can now be derived for given parameter values under specific assumptions about expectations formation about future levels of D and G.

In the following we assume that any change in D or G is expected to be permanent. A government expecting to have its policies reversed would obviously expect its policy changes to be temporary. Such expectations can be captured by an increase in the discount rate, putting more weight on welfare in the near term.

Under the assumption of permanent shifts in G and D, the present value of the government's welfare can be expressed as

$$P_t(w) = [\, a_1D^2(1 - r) + a_2G^2(1 - r) + a_3DG(1 - r) + a_4D + a_5G \,] / r. \qquad \text{(A3)}$$

Maximizing A3, with respect to D (G) at a given level of G (D) leads to the following optimal level of government-induced distortion (insurance) in domestic financial markets:

$$D^* = - [\, a_4 + a_3G\,(1 - r)\,] / 2a_1\,(1 - r)\ (> 0), \qquad \text{(A4)}$$
$$G^* = - [a_5 + a_3\,D\,(1 - r)\,] / 2a_2\,(1 - r)\ (> 0). \qquad \text{(A5)}$$

Next we solve for the simultaneously optimized values of D and G by using the first-order conditions for maximization of (A3), inserting (A4) and (A5) respectively in these conditions.

$$D^{**} = [\, -2a_4a_2 + a_3a_5\,] / [\, 4a_1a_2 - a^2_3\,]\,(1 - r) > 0. \qquad \text{(A6)}$$
$$G^{**} = [\, -2a_5a_1 + a_3a_4\,] / [\, 4a_1a_2 - a^2_3\,]\,(1 - r) > 0. \qquad \text{(A7)}$$

Both D^{**} and G^{**} are positive if $4a_1a_2 > (a_3)^2$. We expect this condition to hold. Using (A4) through (A7) the following results are obtained:

$$\delta D^*/\delta r > 0,\ \delta D^{**}/\delta r > 0,\ \delta G^*/\delta r > 0,\ \delta G^{**}/\delta r > 0 \qquad (A8)$$
$$\delta D^*/\delta a_1 > 0,\ \delta D^{**}/\delta a_1 > 0,\ \delta G^*/\delta a_1 = 0,\ \delta G^{**}/\delta a_1 > 0 \qquad (A9)$$
$$\delta G^*/\delta a_2 > 0,\ \delta G^{**}/\delta a_2 > 0,\ \delta D^*/\delta a_2 = 0,\ \delta D^{**}/\delta a_2 > 0 \qquad (A10)$$
$$\delta D^*/\delta a_3 > 0,\ \delta D^{**}/\delta a_3 > 0,\ \delta G^*/\delta a_3 > 0,\ \delta D^{**}/\delta a_3 > 0 \qquad (A11)$$

Equation (A8) says that as the interest rate rises and the time horizon of the government shortens, optimal levels of distortions and insurance increase. The results in (A9)–(A11) capture effects of capital mobility and capital account convertibility on endogenous levels of distortions and guarantees of financial investment.

We assume the following relationships between the *a*-parameters and capital mobility when *D* takes the form of regulatory intervention in the form of quantitative restrictions and price controls.

ASSUMPTION 1. *Increased capital mobility increases* $|a_1|$ *and leaves* a_4 *unchanged.* Assuming that a certain value of *D* implies that specific goals with respect to, for example, credit allocation are achieved, the distributional objectives are achieved independent of the degree of capital mobility but the efficiency costs of achieving these objectives increase as capital mobility increases. Either exchange regulation must be more encompassing and costly to enforce or the distributional goals are achieved to a lesser extent. Thus, the rate at which efficiency losses increases with distortions increase with higher capital mobility.

ASSUMPTION 2. *Increased capital mobility causes* $|a_2|$ *to increase leaving* a_5 *unchanged.* Defining *G* as a certain level of insurance offered households and firms, the welfare benefit in terms of consumer protection remains unchanged as capital mobility increases. However, the efficiency loss caused by moral hazard at a certain level of insurance increases, because a richer menu of risky investments becomes available. Alternatively, more costly supervision of, for example, banks' asset allocation would be necessary.

ASSUMPTION 3. *Increased capital mobility reduces* a_3, *if* $a_3 > 0$. A certain set of regulatory policies for financial sector asset allocation would be less effective in reducing moral hazard when capital mobility increases. Alternatively, the costs of regulatory policies to achieve a certain degree of reduction in moral hazard would increase. These assumptions and expressions (A9)–(A11) imply that D^*, D^{**}, G^* and G^{**} fall with higher mobility. In other words, capital account liberalization would enhance the credibility of a financial liberalization program under the assumptions made.

Finally, we turn to the government's perception of welfare as capital account liberalization and, by assumption, capital mobility increase. Disregarding that capital account liberalization may have efficiency effects independent of effects on the coefficients in the welfare function (A1), the government can maximize its welfare at a given level of government guarantees by minimizing capital mobility. Thereby, the government obtains the best possible trade-off between distributional gains and efficiency losses under the assumptions stated above.

The result that capital mobility should be minimized is obtained under three important assumptions. First, there is no independent economic efficiency gain due to increased capital mobility. Second, G_t is constant and, third, there are no alternative available means for achieving distributional objectives. Relaxing the second assumption, the expressions for D^{**} and G^{**} are inserted in (A3). Taking the derivative of welfare with respect to a_1 we obtain that

$$\begin{aligned}\delta P_t(w)/\delta a_1 &= D^{**2}(1-r);\ \delta P_t(w)/\delta a_2\\ &= G^{**2}(1-r);\ \delta P_t(w)/\delta a_3\\ &= D^{**}G^{**}(1-r).\end{aligned} \qquad \text{(A12)}$$

The expressions in (A12) imply once again that unless there is an independent welfare gain of increased capital mobility, the government has an incentive to reduce capital mobility as much as possible. Thus, liberalization of capital account transactions would not occur unless there are independent welfare gains from such liberalization.

In the main text, conclusions are drawn under the assumption that an additional term for efficiency losses of restrictions on capital account transactions is included in the welfare function (A1). Such a term would be characterized by increasing marginal efficiency losses of restrictions on convertibility and capital mobility.

Capital Mobility and Government Intervention by Taxes and Subsidies

We assume now that certain distributional objectives are obtained by subsidies and taxes on financial market prices in specific markets. For example, an interest rate subsidy on mortgages can be used to reduce capital costs for housing. In equation (A1), for the government's perception of social welfare the benefits a_4D remain unchanged relative to the case of quantitative restrictions. The parameter a_1 for efficiency losses is reduced in absolute terms, however. We denote the parameters in (A1) a_1^m to a_5^m, when taxes/ subsidies are used instead of direct intervention. The following assumptions are made about the parameters:

$$|a_1^m| < |a_1|\ ,\ a_2^m = a_2,\ a_3^m \geq a_3,\ a_4^m = a_4,\ a_5^m = a_5.$$

The parameters a_1^m and a_4^m have been discussed. The parameters a_2^m and a_5^m remain unchanged, because they refer specifically to government guarantees. If tax/subsidy policies are used to reduce the moral-hazard problem caused by guarantees, then the efficiency gain is increased (or remains unchanged relative to quantitative restrictions being imposed). Thus $a_3^m \geq a_3$.

It follows immediately from (A12) and (A6) above that the government's perception of welfare is higher, when it uses tax/subsidy policies to achieve distributional objectives.

The effects of capital mobility and currency convertibility on the *a*-parameters are most likely the same in direction for tax/subsidy policies as for intervention policies. In order to achieve a certain distributional objective leading to a benefit $a_4^m D$, the government must use stronger tax and subsidy incentives in order to achieve a certain allocation of financial resources when capital mobility is high. The reason is that foreign assets provide a richer menu of substitutes for domestic financial investment.

All results derived above for effects of increased capital mobility hold for tax/subsidy policies, as well as for intervention policies. Another conclusion is that the higher costs of achieving distributional objectives when capital mobility is high can be mitigated by increased use of tax/subsidy policies, as well as by government initiatives to liberalize domestic financial markets further.

Finally, if first-best policy instruments to achieve distributional objectives are available, then the case for distortions and capital account restrictions is weakened. Assume, for example, that taxes and transfers can be used to achieve desirable objectives. The only remaining reason to introduce distortions is that they may counteract moral hazard effects of insurance. Any independent efficiency costs of restricting convertibility makes the case for such restrictions weak.

Notes

1. For analysis and references to other literature on the ups and downs of the dollar, see Arndt, Sweeney, and Willett (1985) and Willett and Wihlborg (1990).

2. We present this view in some detail in Willett and Wihlborg (1990). This paper contains numerous references to the literature on international capital flows and speculative behavior. See also the analysis and references in Baillie and McMahon (1989) and Surajaras and Sweeney (1992).

3. See the analysis and references in Willett (1988) and Persson and Tabellini (1992).

4. Elsewhere we have raised questions about the effectiveness of pegged exchange rates; on this score see Burdekin, Westbrook, and Willett (1993) and Wihlborg and Willett (1991,1993).

5. See Wooley (1992) and Shafer (1995).

6. See Calvo, Leiderman, and Reinhart (1995) for a discussion of the effects of economic conditions in the industrialized countries on capital flows to developing countries.

7. See, for example, de Cecco and Giavazzi (1994) and Walters (1986).

8. Although we do not want to make too much of it, there is even a political economy argument that could lead in some circumstances to a case for liberalizing the capital account before domestic financial markets. Suppose that there is a strong split in views within a government about whether liberalization would be desirable. Assume further that the reformers have primary control of international policy and the status quo advocates have control of domestic policy. By opening the capital account, the international group could greatly raise the cost to the domestic groups of, for example, maintaining regulated interest rates, and hence increase the pressure for domestic liberalization. From such a political economy perspective, the adoption of some policies with greater short-run economic costs could help stimulate the adoption of better policies over the longer run.

9. See, for example, Edwards and Edwards (1991) and Chapter 3 by Wihlborg and Dezseri in this volume.

10. See Chulan, Perez-Quiros and Popper (1996) and Frankel and Rose (1996). See Claessens, Dooley, and Warner (1995) for a different view.

11. Increased net capital inflows imply that the current account deteriorates correspondingly. By macroeconomic identities, a deterioration in the current account implies an increase in investment in excess of savings. Thus, the capital inflow may either increase investment or reduce savings (increase consumption).

12. Experience has made many observers more dubious about the ability of governments to run activist policies in a second-best world, i.e., about their ability to impose optimal distortions in some sectors to offset exogenous distortions in other sectors. In fact, the initial distortions were often put in place by the government.

13. We have not seen the argument for a dynamic process favoring liberalization being compared to Hayek's dynamics of increasingly widespread regulatory involvement by governments. The analogy was first pointed out to us by a Claremont Ph.D. student, Alex Huemer. The economic liberalization program in New Zealand in the mid- and late 1980s described in Colin (1992) presents an excellent example of the process of liberalization. Asilis and Milesi-Ferretti (1994) survey the recent literature on the political sustainability of reforms. Murphy, Shleifer and Vishny (1992) and Dewatripont and Roland (1993) analyze the political stability of partial reform programs.

14. Wihlborg (1993) contains a political economy analysis (in Swedish) of Swedish exchange controls since 1945 and their removal in the late 1980s.

15. For example, the benefits to households of deposit insurance begin as soon as the program starts. One way to interpret the time lag for efficiency losses is that enforcement costs for the regulation to achieve desired objectives increase as households and firms learn to avoid the regulation.

16. This result is not perfectly general but depends on the magnitude of the interdependence between the government's interventions for egalitarian and insurance objectives. The result can be reversed if the interaction effect is very strong.

References

Arndt, Sven, Richard J. Sweeney, and Thomas D. Willett, eds. 1985. *Exchange Rates, Trade, and the U.S. Economy.* Cambridge, Mass.: Ballinger.

Asilis, Carlos M., and Gian Maria Milesi-Ferretti. 1994. "On the Political Sustainability of Economic Reform." *IMF Paper on Policy Analysis and Assessment*, No. 94/3. Washington, D.C.: International Monetary Fund, January.

Baillie, Richard, and Patrick McMahon. 1989. *The Foreign Exchange Market: Theory and Econometric Evidence.* Cambridge: Cambridge University Press.

Banaian, King, Richard C.K. Burdekin, and Thomas D. Willett. "On the Political Economy of Central Bank Independence," in K.D. Hoover and S.M. Sheffrin, eds., *Monetarism and the Methodology of Economics: Essays in Honor of Thomas Mayer*. London: Edward Elgar, forthcoming.

Burdekin, Richard C.K., Jilleen R. Westbrook, Thomas D. Willett. 1993. "Exchange Rate Pegging as a Disinflation Strategy: Evidence from the European Monetary System," in Pierre L. Siklos, ed., *Varieties of Monetary Reform: Lessons and Experiences on the Road to Monetary Union*. Pp. 45–71. Amsterdam: Kluwer Academic Publishers.

Calvo, Guillermo, Leonardo Leiderman, and Carmen Reinhart. 1995. "Capital Inflows to Latin America with Reference to the Asian Experience," in Sebastian Edwards, ed., *Capital Controls, Exchange Rates, and Monetary Policy in the World Economy*. Pp. 339–82. Cambridge: Cambridge University Press.

de Cecco, Marcello, and Francesco Giavazzi. 1994. "Italy's Experience Within and Without the European Monetary System," in J. Wijnholds, S. Effinger, and L. Hoggduin, eds., *A Frameworkfor Monetary Stability*. Pp. 221–238. Dordrecht: Kluwer.

Chulan, P., Gabriel Perez-Quiros, and Helen Popper. 1996. "International Capital Flows: Do Short-Term Investment and Direct Investment Differ?" Unpublished manuscript.

Claessens, Stijn, Michael P. Dooley, and Andrew Warner. 1995. "Portfolio Capital Flows: Hot or Cold?" *World Bank Economic Review* 9(1): 153–74.

Colin, James. 1992. *New Territory: The Transformation of New Zealand 1984–92.* Wellington, NZ: Bridget Williams Books Ltd.

Dewatripont, Mathias, and Gerald Roland. 1993. "The Design of Reform Packages in Eastern Europe." *CEPR Discussion Paper* No. 860, November.

Edwards, Sebastian, ed. 1995. *Capital Controls, Exchange Rates, and Monetary Policy in the World Economy*. Cambridge: Cambridge University Press.

Edwards, Sebastian, and Alejandra C. Edwards. 1991. *Monetarism and Liberalization: The Chilean Experiment*. Reprint. Chicago: Chicago University Press.

———. 1992. "Markets and Democracy: Lessons from Chile." *World Economy* 15(2), March: 203–19.

Frenkel, Jacob. 1982. "The Order of Economic Liberalization: A Comment," in Karl Brunner and Allen Meltzer, eds., *Economic Policy in a World of Change*. Pp. 199–201. Carnegie Rochester Conference Series. Amsterdam: North Holland.

———. 1983. "Panel Discussion on the Southern Cone." *IMF Staff Papers* 30(1): 164–73.

Frankel, Jacob, and Andrew Rose. 1996. "Currency Crashes in Emerging Markets." *International Finance Discussion Papers* No. 534. Washington, D.C.: Board of Governors of the Federal Reserve, September.

Friedman, Milton. 1953. "The Case for Flexible Exchange Rates," in *Essays in Positive Economics*. Pp. 157–203. Chicago: Chicago University Press.

Green, Joshua E., and Peter Isard. 1991. *Currency Convertibility and the Transformation of Centrally Planned Economies*. Washington D.C.: International Monetary Fund.

Guitián, Manuel. 1995. "Capital Account Liberalization: Bringing Policy in Line with Reality," in Sebastian Edwards, ed., *Capital Controls, Exchange Rates, and Monetary Policy in the World Economy*. Pp. 71–92. Cambridge: Cambridge University Press.

Hanson, James. 1995. "Opening the Capital Account: Costs, Benefits, and Sequencing," in Sebastian Edwards, ed., *Capital Controls, Exchange Rates, and Monetary Policy in the World Economy*. Pp. 393–419. Cambridge: Cambridge University Press.

Hayek, Friedrich von. 1960. *The Constitution of Liberty*. Chicago: Chicago University Press.

Krueger, Anne O. 1984. "Problems of Liberalization," in Arnold Harberger, ed., *World Economic Growth*. Pp. 403–23. San Francisco: ICS Press.

McKinnon, Ronald. 1991. *The Order of Economic Liberalization*. Baltimore: Johns Hopkins University Press.

Murphy, Kevin M., Andrei Shleifer, and Robert W. Vishny. 1992. "The Transition to a Market Economy: Pitfalls of Partial Reform." *Quarterly Journal of Economics*, August: 889–906.

Persson, Torsten, and Guido Tabellini. 1990. *Macroeconomic Policy, Credibility and Politics*. London: Harwood Academic.

Shafer, R. 1995. "Experience with Controls on International Capital Movements in OECD Countries: Solution or Problem for Monetary Policy," in Sebastian Edwards, ed., *Capital Controls, Exchange Rates, and Monetary Policy in the World Economy*. Pp. 393–419. Cambridge: Cambridge University Press.

Surajaras, Patchara, and Richard J. Sweeney. 1992. *Profit-Making Speculation in Foreign Exchange Markets*. Boulder, Colo: Westview Press.

Walters, Alan. 1986. *Britain's Economic Renaissance: Margaret Thatcher's Reforms, 1979–1984*. New York: Oxford University Press.

Wihlborg, Clas G. 1993. "Valutaregleringen," in Lars Werin, ed., *Från ränteregler-ing till inflationsnorm*. Ch. 11. Stockholm: SNS förlag.

Wihlborg, Clas G., and Thomas D. Willett. 1991. "Optimal Currency Areas Revisited," in Clas G. Wihlborg, Michele Fratianni and Thomas D. Willett, eds., *Financial Regulation and Monetary Arrangements After 1992*. Pp. 279–97. Amsterdam: North Holland.

———. 1993. "The Instability of Half-Way Measures in the Transition to a Common Currency," in Herbert Grubel, ed., *EC 1992—Perspectives from the Outside*. London: Macmillan.

Willett, Thomas D., ed. 1988. *Political Business Cycles: The Political Economy of Money, Inflation, and Unemployment*. Durham, N.C.: Duke University Press for the Pacific Research Institute.

Willett, Thomas D., and King Banaian. forthcoming. "Currency Substitution and Seignorage Consideration in the Choice of Currency Policies," in Paul Mizen and Eric Pentecost, eds., *The Macroeconomics of International Currencies*. London: Edward Elgar.

Willett, Thomas D., and Clas G. Wihlborg. 1990. "International Capital Flows, the Dollar, and U.S. Financial Policies," in William Haraf and Thomas D. Willett, eds., *Monetary Policy for a Volatile World Economy*. Pp. 51–88. Washington, D.C.: American Enterprise Institute for Public Policy Research.

Woo, Wing. 1994. "The Art of Reforming Centrally Planned Economies: Comparing China, Poland and Russia." *Journal of Comparative Economics*, June: 276–308.

Wooley, John T. 1992. "Policy Credibility and European Monetary Institutions," in Alberta M. Sbragia, ed., *Euro-Politics: Institutions and Policymaking in the New European Community*. Pp. 157–90. Washington, D.C.: Brookings Institute.

8

A Payments Mechanism for the Independent States of the Former Soviet Union

Michael Dooley

Introduction: Economic Rationale for a Payments Mechanism

The transition to a market-oriented economy means that decentralized decisions by households and firms are organized by market forces. Because such decisions are not perfectly synchronized over time, market-determined trade in goods and services across national boundaries generates credit positions among the traders and among aggregates of traders defined by national residence. The basic requirement for an international payments system is that credits acceptable to exporters are available to importers. In a closed economy such as the former Soviet Union, residents of each republic accepted ruble-denominated liabilities of domestic banks in trade with residents of other republics. In the international context, transactions across national borders are settled with an acceptable credit instrument, for example a U.S. dollar or ECU-denominated liability of an international bank. To the extent that ruble-denominated bank liabilities are not generally accepted in interstate trade, an alternative settlement system is needed to avoid a barter system. Because residents of the former Soviet republics do not have access to international credit markets, settlement in foreign currencies would require the accumulation of a stock of international money through trade surpluses with the West.

The stock of money needed to facilitate trade depends upon the willingness of transactors to extend credit to one another. In a well-functioning payments system, credit markets allow individual traders to economize on cash balances by keeping track of debit and credit positions and making cash payments only after all possible netting of bilateral payments. In an international payments mechanism the same netting of payments is accomplished in the foreign exchange markets and international credit markets.

The basic economic rationale for a payments mechanism for the transition economies in Eastern Europe and the Commonwealth of Independent States is the same as for any other market-oriented trading system. Since individual decisions to buy and sell are decentralized in any arbitrary time period there will be a net credit or debit position for any group of transactors grouped by national residence. The benefits of a decentralized market-oriented system are what the transition is all about. But this system will require a payments mechanism which did not exist under the previous central planning regime. There was, of course, something that looked like a payments system, but the value of the "credit" positions in the system was ultimately determined by the central plan's ability to force participants to deliver goods and services in exchange for credits. This chapter assumes that a "market-oriented" payments mechanism will develop slowly if left to itself and assesses the role, if any, for government involvement. In particular, the case for an arrangement in which a payments mechanism makes credits available to facilitate interstate trade is explored and given some empirical content.

I start from the premise that the Commonwealth's members have a strong mutual interest in maintaining trade among themselves. Although it is clear that the pattern of trade inherited from the command economy is quite different from what will eventually emerge under market forces, it is also clear that the optimal speed of adjustment is not infinite. The preferred role for a payments mechanism is that it be neutral in the sense that it neither speeds the transition by discouraging interstate trade nor artificially maintains patterns of trade inherited from central planning.

The working assumption for this chapter is that a private credit market will not develop overnight to facilitate interstate trade to the same extent that trade outside the area is facilitated. An important restraint to interstate trade at this time is that the newly independent states are not seen as good credit risks by one another. This problem is particularly acute in the early days of the transition because no one knows what pattern of credit balances will evolve as trade is reoriented by market forces. Moreover, it is difficult to know how governments might react to imbalances with other states. Thus, the usual mechanisms for trade finance, including credit from commercial banks or government agencies, are not available for interstate trade.

There is no doubt that the existing trade pattern within the Commonwealth states and Eastern Europe will undergo difficult adjustments over the next few years. This will occur with or without a functioning payments mechanism. Without a payments mechanism the speed of "adjustment" will be determined by the ability of the states to arrange and manage a barter system or a system based on foreign currency settlements. If this implies a collapse of trade there is a strong possibility that the welfare costs of the transition will be larger than they need to be. Developments thus far in 1992 in the Commonwealth of Independent States and recent experience in Eastern Europe suggest that interstate trade is shrinking very rapidly. At the present time, trade among republics is increasingly conducted through barter, even though all the Commonwealth's members remain in the ruble area. Moreover, controls on exports at the republic level invite retaliation and mutually destructive policies.

In contrast, for trade involving a resident of a transition economy and the rest of the world, one of the parties typically does have access to private and, in most cases, official financing. Thus, it seems clear that, other things being equal, trade within the region is at a disadvantage to trade with the outside. Thus, a payments mechanism is not a device to subsidize interstate trade and would not be detrimental to the appropriate development of trade with the rest of the world. There is no doubt that given the importance of integrating these economies into the world market it would be a mistake to encourage or subsidize the inefficient trade patterns inherited from central planning. This chapter explores the opposite possibility. It is possible that the provision of a payments mechanism is necessary to overcome an initial distortion that reduces trade among these countries during the transition to a level below what would occur on an "even playing field."

The obvious analogies between postwar Europe and the economies in transition have led a number of observers to reconsider a payments union as a possible interim arrangement for organizing and financing trade within the region (Dornbusch 1991, Gros 1991, Havrylyshen and Williamson 1991, and Kenen 1991). Although there seems to be considerable interest in these matters outside official circles, the reaction to date from the Russian government and international organizations has been cool to hostile. It is perhaps not surprising that the Russian government would prefer to maintain a ruble zone assuming that they could put in place a mechanism for controlling credits to governments of other states. Indeed, the Russian central bank is reportedly putting in place a system that will allow it to keep track of and limit net credit to other states (Williamson 1992). However, in this environment it seems likely that a growing list of states will opt for an independent currency. In this event, difficult decisions will have to be made concerning the exchange and trade arrangements among these economies.

The official preferred evolution of the payments mechanism is a "back to the future" scenario in which prices are decontrolled, trade is free, fiscal policies are coordinated, ruble payments are generally accepted and transfers among the political subdivisions are automatically financed or eliminated. While this is perhaps the "first-best" solution to the current difficulties, it seems likely that some Commonwealth states may be unwilling or unable to participate in a ruble area with these characteristics.

If the first-best solution is infeasible, independent states would still have a strong economic interest in pooling their mutual risks and their limited foreign exchange reserves in order to maintain the highest possible level of balanced trade among themselves. Imbalances in trade among the regions will develop, especially early in the adjustment period, but it is not necessary to wait until a fully articulated and financed adjustment mechanism is in place before proceeding with a mechanism to finance roughly balanced trade. Surely, balanced trade at a level constrained by limited financing arrangements within the payments mechanism is preferred to the realistic alternative of balanced trade constrained by barter and protection.

The mechanics of a payments mechanism are straightforward and are presented in detail below. The basic idea is that exports of goods and services pay for imports of goods and services and the payments mechanism should get in the way as little as possible. Members of the mechanism agree to extend credit to other members on well-defined terms and with well-defined credit ceilings. The main theoretical point is that the transactions demand for trade credit or alternative settlement assets is directly related to the value of trade. If the marginal cost of participating in a payments system is high states will choose low trade volumes—a choice they seem to be making now. Thus, government interference is justified by the apparent failure of the market to provide a low-cost alternative mechanism.

An important conceptual question to be addressed in evaluating a payments mechanism is why the credit of the mechanism would be acceptable when the credit of members is not? It is clear that the main risk in extending credit across state borders at the present time is that the government will limit the exports necessary to liquidate the credit. Part of the answer is that the risk of an individual republic refusing to honor its liabilities to the mechanism (by limiting exports) is independent of the risk that other independent states would do the same. Thus, each republic would see the gains from trade as dominating the risk that it would be asked to accept a share of the cost of an individual state's default. Moreover, the export performance of each member would be carefully monitored by their trading partners and this would tend to discourage policies that limit exports.

Western assistance could provide an additional cushion in the form of paid-in capital or credit lines. By helping to maintain economic activity within the mechanism, and by freeing scarce foreign exchange reserves to support trade with the West, donors would help protect their own trading interests in the region. Finally, the payments mechanism would provide timely information about members' trade balances within the region so that credit risks could be limited to levels acceptable to participants. As discussed below, it is likely that large imbalances will develop following the establishment of a clearing mechanism. This does not imply that the system would break down. To the contrary, early information about the initial position of various participants would provide a solid basis for mobilizing credit from outside the formal framework of the mechanism itself. Such credit could be provided by republics with initial surpluses or by nonmember governments and international organizations.

To provide a rough estimate of the resources required to establish a payments mechanism for the Commonwealth, a detailed analysis of historical data for inter-republic trade is provided below. The data suggests that the Commonwealth states would need credit lines or quotas in a mechanism with a value of at least US$30 billion. Western assistance to capitalize the mechanism would be some fraction, perhaps 10 percent, of this amount. The calculations are based, in part, on a rule of thumb that countries hold reserves or credit lines equal to 30 percent of imports to facilitate international trade. This was the size of quotas in the European Payments Union and is the reserve-to-import ratio today for developing countries. If resources of this magnitude are not available, a smaller mechanism would still be useful.

Mechanics

The primary responsibility of the clearing union would be to enforce strict ceilings on debit positions of individual members. Net debt to the mechanism would be limited to some fraction of a year's imports from the group's members. The objective is to provide exporters with a claim on the clearing union rather than the importer or his government. The mechanism described here assumes that a free market for ECU-denominated liabilities of the mechanism determines the exchange rate between the mechanism's ECUs and the national currencies of member countries. The same mechanism could accommodate a fixed exchange rate system in which exporters would be obliged to surrender their ECU positions for domestic currency.

A typical sequence of transactions would be the following:

1. To get the system started, an importer in country A offers to sell domestic currency, or a trade bill, to his central bank for an ECU position in the payments mechanism. The central bank in A "borrows" ECUs from the mechanism and transfers the mechanism ECUs to the importer.

2. The exporter in B exchanges goods for the mechanism ECUs and is required to deposit the mechanism ECUs at his central bank, B. The central bank can either purchase the ECUs for domestic currency at an announced price or it can issue a voucher that the exporter can sell on an open market to a potential importer. The voucher would earn no interest and could be sold to anyone at a market price. (Individual members could organize the domestic market for ECUs to fit their circumstances).
3. Central bank B deposits the ECUs at the mechanism and is now in a position to finance an import into country B. An importer in B sells domestic currency to the central bank, or to the holder of an ECU voucher. Although anyone can hold the voucher, the central bank is only obliged to transfer its ECUs to legitimate importers.
4. An exporter in A exchanges goods for mechanism ECUs and is required to deposit them in his central bank A.
5. Central bank A repays its ECU loan from the mechanism.
6. At the end of each month, or perhaps more frequently, the mechanism adds up credits and debits for each independent state and strikes a multilateral balance. Depending on each member's cumulative position in the mechanism, net positions would be settled first with credit and then increasingly with hard currencies. A member that had reached its quota ceiling would settle entirely with hard currencies. Table 8.1 shows the schedule initially utilized in the EPU.

The *net* credit position of the member central banks would depend upon the normal seasonal and random pattern of exports and imports with other republics. A credit limit might be set at a level equal to four months imports from mechanism members during the previous three years. Net credit positions exceeding this ceiling would be presumed to reflect an imbalance for which financing would be found outside the administration of the mechanism. The mechanism would simply inform the member that further credit was unavailable until its net debit position in the mechanism was reduced.

If, for example, the deficit member had a trade surplus with nonunion countries, or could borrow outside the mechanism, it would be free to use hard currencies to buy mechanism ECUs from voucher holders at market prices in order to restore its position in the mechanism. If the member could not earn or borrow hard currencies, it would have to take other policy actions to encourage exports. Moreover, other international organizations might extend conditional credits.

It would not be necessary for these ECUs to be freely convertible for member governments on demand. The mechanism ECU would normally

TABLE 8.1 Illustrative Scale for Settlement in Hard Currency

Cumulated Imbalances Relative to Quota	*Proportion to Be Settled in Hard Currency* Debtors	*Creditors*
	(in percent)	
0 - 20	–	50
20 - 40	20	50
40 - 60	40	50
60 - 80	60	50
80 - 100	80	50
beyond 100	100	50

trade at a small discount relative to ECU-dominated claims on commercial banks. The acceptability of the ECUs would be enhanced if limited convertibility was backed by paid-in capital of the mechanism. Thus an initial contribution or guarantee of assets by Western governments would be very helpful. The market value of the mechanism ECU would be related to expectations about the long-run value of credit balances at the mechanism. A capital contribution of 10 percent of the maximum net exposure of the mechanism to member states might be enough to maintain the market value of mechanism ECUs.

Nevertheless, it should be remembered that our main objective is to provide a means of payment backed by the member states' ability to produce goods and services for export and their willingness to allow domestic producers to sell to other Commonwealth states. Although the system proposed involves an administrative apparatus, it relies ultimately on the willingness of the republics to allow trade at market prices.

Inter-Republic Trade

Table 8.2 shows a full direction of trade matrix for inter-republic trade for 1987. The basic data for this table are ruble payments at domestic prices. Two important transformations are necessary in order to make the data useful in evaluating trading patterns that might emerge in the first year of a payments mechanism.

The first important problem is to transform the relative prices for imports and exports from each republic to reflect the relative prices that would emerge as domestic relative prices move toward world relative prices. We have guesses about world prices expressed in 1987 rubles for a disaggregated list of exports and imports for each republic. A revaluation of inter-republic trade using these estimates mainly changes the bilateral balance between Russia and all the other republics: the Russian inter-republic trade

TABLE 8.2 Bilateral Trade: Republics' Export and Import of Products for 1987 (domestic prices in millions of rubles)

	Exporting Republic					
Importing Republic	*Russia*	*Ukraine*	*Belarus*	*Uzbekistan*	*Kazakhstan*	*Georgia*
Russia	0.0	25393.3	10279.0	4659.1	4855.9	3130.0
Ukraine	26414.4	0.0	2834.7	782.2	780.6	677.1
Belarus	8844.3	2719.8	0.0	179.4	302.1	226.1
Uzbekistan	5860.4	1501.1	521.4	0.0	1126.1	258.0
Kazakhstan	8881.0	1555.1	778.6	565.2	0.0	340.8
Georgia	2676.2	895.1	271.2	58.8	105.4	0.0
Azerbaijan	2238.9	886.5	285.4	60.0	248.5	141.7
Lithuania	3804.3	676.2	567.1	46.0	66.5	100.5
Moldova	2387.8	1465.9	388.1	97.0	50.9	42.3
Latvia	2475.2	534.7	430.5	34.6	82.8	95.4
Kyrgyzstan	1341.3	291.6	143.1	295.8	271.4	80.6
Tajikistan	1384.8	415.5	150.2	397.4	239.0	78.4
Armenia	1632.2	528.8	275.8	72.6	39.3	101.1
Turkmenia	1172.6	438.3	100.5	159.5	112.1	85.3
Estonia	1740.6	426.6	202.2	50.5	56.7	29.2
Total Inter-republic Exports	70854.0	37728.5	17227.8	7458.1	8337.3	5386.5
Exports Abroad	31855.9	6269.2	1636.3	1515.8	473.8	356.6
Total Exports	102709.9	43997.7	18864.1	8973.9	8811.1	5743.1

(*continued*)

TABLE 8.2 (*continued*)

	Exporting Republic					
Importing Republic	*Azerbaijan*	*Lithuania*	*Moldova*	*Latvia*	*Kyrgyzstan*	*Tajikistan*
Russia	3749.5	2923.2	3203.1	2153.8	852.1	929.5
Ukraine	738.2	712.6	995.6	692.3	251.5	206.0
Belarus	240.4	468.1	275.6	332.5	117.0	55.2
Uzbekistan	186.5	180.0	72.2	127.8	412.8	257.9
Kazakhstan	284.8	172.7	171.3	203.0	230.0	246.1
Georgia	318.4	74.0	96.3	98.1	26.1	14.9
Azerbaijan	0.0	57.7	61.0	64.7	36.4	44.0
Lithuania	33.8	0.0	99.2	245.5	71.1	27.1
Moldova	41.0	88.1	0.0	72.4	23.4	6.8
Latvia	38.3	489.7	152.2	0.0	31.2	9.9
Kyrgyzstan	44.8	47.4	47.8	27.8	0.0	66.0
Tajikistan	92.5	32.9	27.1	32.7	97.3	0.0
Armenia	333.1	59.3	93.2	54.6	30.9	12.7
Turkmenia	164.4	43.0	28.4	29.2	77.9	70.7
Estonia	25.1	109.4	76.4	178.2	10.9	22.8
Total Inter-republic Exports	6290.8	5458.1	5399.4	4312.6	2268.6	1969.9
Exports Abroad	471.6	412.2	227.8	380.9	710.1	294.3
Total Exports	6762.4	5870.3	5627.2	4693.5	2978.7	2264.2

(*continued*)

TABLE 8.2 (*continued*)

	Exporting Republic			*Total Inter-republic*	*Imports from*	*Total*
	Armenia	*Turkmenia*	*Estonia*	*Imports*	*Abroad*	*Imports*
Russia	2255.8	1168.7	1652.4	67205.7	64264.3	131470.0
Ukraine	551.0	175.4	357.1	36168.7	14011.5	50180.2
Belarus	138.6	48.8	135.0	14082.9	3624.2	17707.1
Uzbekistan	163.8	658.2	47.3	11373.5	1599.9	12973.4
Kazakhstan	171.7	67.3	100.7	13768.3	2583.7	16352.0
Georgia	132.5	10.2	32.7	4809.9	1258.7	6068.6
Azerbaijan	92.9	5.5	27.7	4250.9	1302.4	5553.3
Lithuania	43.4	10.8	68.0	5859.5	1108.5	6968.0
Moldova	46.1	11.5	44.4	4765.7	1148.9	5914.6
Latvia	33.2	23.4	195.0	4626.1	967.2	5593.3
Kyrgyzstan	64.6	45.9	12.8	2780.9	710.1	3491.0
Tajikistan	47.5	67.9	14.0	3077.2	373.9	3451.1
Armenia	0.0	12.5	35.7	3281.8	788.5	4070.3
Turkmenia	105.8	0.0	8.2	2595.9	328.3	2924.2
Estonia	23.4	21.2	0.0	2973.2	660.5	3633.7
Commonwealth				181620.2	94730.6	276350.8
Total Inter-republic Exports	3870.3	2327.3	2731.0	181620.2		
Exports Abroad	66.4	120.2	213.8	45004.9		
Total Exports	3936.7	2447.5	2944.8	226625.1		

surplus rises from about R4.4 billion to R28.6 billion. Inspection of the disaggregated data indicates that less than half of the increase in the Russian surplus, R11.4 billion, is accounted for by a revaluation of energy prices. The remaining R12.8 billion is mainly accounted for by assigning lower world prices to Russian imports from other republics.

These estimates were made at the request of Union authorities who were interested at the time in demonstrating that republics other than Russia had a strong interest in remaining in the Union. This may or may not have influenced the results, but it would seem prudent to consider the implied transfer from the Russian Republic as an upper bound. A reasonable alternative might be to incorporate the estimates for world prices for energy on the grounds that these would have been easy to measure but to exclude the estimated price adjustments for other goods.

Table 8.3 shows a direction of trade matrix based on these assumptions. The absolute measure is still rubles and "world" prices for oil are translated at the official exchange rate of R1 = $1.60. Using this table we can start to analyze patterns of inter-republic trade. Some obvious features include:

1. For all the Commonwealth states trade within the area is much more important than trade with countries outside the area.
2. All the Commonwealth states are highly open to inter-republic trade.
3. While trade in oil and gas is important, even when valued at world prices it accounts for only 26 percent of Russian exports and 17 percent of total inter-republic trade.

Table 8.4 shows the bilateral trade balances for each republic with all other republics derived from Table 8.3. This data can help quantify two issues. The first is the potential savings in clearing balances that would be realized by multilateral netting among the republics. If each republic had to settle its bilateral deficits with assets, the volume of transactions would be equal to the sum of all the negative entries in Table 8.4. For example, Ukraine would owe about R3.1 billion. If the same transactions were first netted in a multilateral union, Ukraine would make no payments in this year. Instead its account would be credited with about R13.8 billion. For the system, payments would be reduced by about 40 percent with multilateral netting. The percentage savings would increase if the dominant net surplus position of Russia was less in the new system that it is estimated to have been in 1987.

The second important issue is the size of credit limits that would have been required within the mechanism to finance the imbalances estimated for 1987. I first do the exercise in terms of rubles because the appropriate translation into dollars is a separate problem. Table 8.5 shows the bilateral

TABLE 8.3 Bilateral Trade Adjusted for World Energy Prices: Republics' Export and Import of Products for 1987 (millions of rubles)

	Exporting Republic					
Importing Republic	*Russia*	*Ukraine*	*Belarus*	*Uzbekistan*	*Kazakhstan*	*Georgia*
Russia	0.00	25542.54	11066.64	5218.68	5345.76	3137.98
Ukraine	31493.32	0.00	3229.22	796.34	785.92	681.58
Belarus	11248.94	2754.66	0.00	180.38	302.80	226.24
Uzbekistan	6318.06	1505.02	521.52	0.00	1217.52	258.00
Kazakhstan	10660.54	1555.94	779.16	610.98	0.00	340.80
Georgia	3007.30	897.06	273.86	59.50	105.40	0.00
Azerbaijan	2608.08	891.26	304.16	60.42	478.10	141.70
Lithuania	5002.14	687.12	779.20	46.42	66.50	100.50
Moldova	2701.68	1833.68	419.46	98.12	50.90	42.30
Latvia	2758.14	551.64	548.10	35.02	82.80	95.40
Kyrgyzstan	1566.56	291.74	143.10	376.16	359.46	80.60
Tajikistan	1550.98	415.78	150.20	500.86	313.76	78.40
Armenia	1832.68	529.08	276.64	72.60	39.30	102.78
Turkmenia	1189.40	438.44	100.50	165.10	116.86	85.30
Estonia	2059.80	429.12	224.04	50.64	56.70	29.20
Total Inter-republic Exports	83997.62	38323.08	18816.1	8271.22	9321.78	5400.78
Exports abroad	31855.90	6269.20	1636.3	1515.80	473.80	356.6
Total Exports	115853.52	44592.28	20452.4	9787.02	9795.58	5757.38

(*continued*)

TABLE 8.3 (*continued*)

	Exporting Republic					
Importing Republic	*Azerbaijan*	*Lithuania*	*Moldova*	*Latvia*	*Kyrgyzstan*	*Tajikistan*
Russia	4453.98	2991.94	3203.8	2161.50	852.1	929.8
Ukraine	764.94	714.42	995.6	693.4	251.5	206.0
Belarus	244.18	475.52	275.6	332.9	117.0	55.2
Uzbekistan	187.34	180.00	72.2	128.2	414.3	285.9
Kazakhstan	295.72	172.84	171.3	203.0	230.0	246.1
Georgia	529.52	74.00	96.3	98.1	26.1	14.9
Azerbaijan	0.00	57.70	61.0	64.7	36.4	44.0
Lithuania	34.08	0.00	99.2	247.9	71.1	27.1
Moldova	41.14	88.10	0.0	72.5	23.4	6.8
Latvia	38.30	752.62	152.2	0.0	31.2	9.9
Kyrgyzstan	44.94	47.40	47.8	27.8	0.0	66.0
Tajikistan	123.16	32.90	27.1	32.7	97.3	0.0
Armenia	629.76	59.30	93.2	54.6	30.9	12.7
Turkmenia	277.38	43.00	28.4	29.2	77.9	70.7
Estonia	25.24	130.82	76.4	178.2	10.9	22.8
Total Inter-republic Exports	7689.68	5820.6	5400.1	4324.8	2270.14	1997.9
Exports Abroad	471.60	412.2	227.8	380.9	710.10	294.3
Total Exports	8161.28	6232.8	5627.9	4705.7	2980.24	2292.2

(*continued*)

TABLE 8.3 (*continued*)

		Exporting Republic		*Total*	*Imports*	
Importing Republic	*Armenia*	*Turkmenia*	*Estonia*	*Inter-republic Imports*	*from Abroad*	*Total Imports*
Russia	2255.8	1387.9	1660.9	70209.40	64563.3	134772.74
Ukraine	551.1	191.8	357.1	41712.28	14074.2	55786.50
Belarus	138.6	48.8	135.0	16535.84	3626.6	20162.42
Uzbekistan	163.8	1403.4	47.3	12702.94	1656.6	14359.54
Kazakhstan	171.7	75.7	100.7	15614.48	2583.7	18198.18
Georgia	132.5	10.2	32.7	5357.44	1299.6	6657.02
Azerbaijan	92.9	5.5	27.7	4873.62	1303.5	6177.14
Lithuania	43.4	10.8	68.0	7283.44	1109.2	8392.64
Moldova	46.1	11.5	44.4	5480.12	1148.9	6629.02
Latvia	33.2	23.4	195.1	5307.06	967.2	6274.26
Kyrgyzstan	64.6	60.6	12.8	3189.56	710.1	3899.66
Tajikistan	47.5	103.6	14.0	3488.24	373.9	3862.14
Armenia	0.0	12.5	35.7	3781.74	788.5	4570.24
Turkmenia	105.8	0.0	8.2	2736.18	328.3	3064.48
Estonia	23.4	21.2	0.0	3338.46	660.5	3998.96
Commonwealth				201610.80	95194.1	296804.94
Total Inter-republic Exports	3870.44	3366.94	2739.68	201610.8		
Exports Abroad	66.4	120.2	213.80	45004.9		
Total Exports	3936.84	3487.14	2953.48	246615.7		

TABLE 8.4 Bilateral Balances and Net and Gross Settlement: Republics' Export and Import of Products for 1987 (millions of rubles)

	Exporting Republic					
Importing Republic	*Russia*	*Ukraine*	*Belarus*	*Uzbekistan*	*Kazakhstan*	*Georgia*
Russia	0.00	-5950.78	-182.30	-1099.38	-5314.78	130.7
Ukraine	5950.78	0.00	474.56	-708.68	-770.02	-215.5
Belarus	182.30	-474.56	0.00	-341.44	-476.36	47.6
Uzbekistan	1099.38	708.68	341.44	0.00	606.54	198.5
Kazakhstan	5314.78	770.02	476.36	-606.54	0.00	235.4
Georgia	-130.68	215.48	47.62	-198.50	-235.40	0.0
Azerbaijan	-1845.90	126.32	59.98	-126.92	182.38	-387.8
Lithuania	2010.20	-27.30	303.68	-133.58	-106.34	26.5
Moldova	-502.12	838.08	143.86	25.92	-120.40	-54.0
Latvia	596.64	-141.78	215.18	-93.20	-120.20	-2.7
Kyrgyzstan	714.46	40.24	26.10	-38.18	129.46	54.5
Tajikistan	621.18	209.78	95.00	214.96	67.66	63.5
Armenia	-423.12	-22.06	138.04	-91.20	-132.40	-29.7
Turkmenia	-198.54	246.66	51.70	-1238.32	41.16	75.1
Estonia	398.86	72.02	89.04	3.34	-44.00	-3.5
Without Clearing	3100.0	6616 .0	182.0	4676.0	7320.0	741.0
With Clearing	0.0	3389.0	0.0	4431.0	6292.0	0.0

(*continued*)

TABLE 8.4 (*continued*)

	Exporting Republic					
Importing Republic	*Azerbaijan*	*Lithuania*	*Moldova*	*Latvia*	*Kyrgyzstan*	*Tajikistan*
Russia	1845.90	-2010.2	502.1	-596.6	-714.5	-621.28
Ukraine	-126.32	27.3	-838.1	141.8	-40.2	-209.8
Belarus	-59.98	-303.7	-143.9	-215.2	-26.1	-95.0
Uzbekistan	126.92	133.6	-25.9	93.2	39.2	-215.0
Kazakhstan	-182.38	106.3	120.4	120.2	-129.5	67.7
Georgia	387.82	-26.5	54.0	2.7	-54.5	-63.5
Azerbaijan	0.00	23.6	19.9	26.4	-8.5	-79.2
Lithuania	-23.62	0.0	11.1	-504.7	23.7	-5.8
Moldova	-19.86	-11.1	0.0	-79.7	-24.4	-20.3
Latvia	-26.40	504.7	79.7	0.0	3.4	-22.8
Kyrgyzstan	8.54	-23.7	24.4	-3.4	0.0	-31.3
Tajikistan	79.16	5.8	20.3	22.8	31.3	0.0
Armenia	536.86	15.9	47.1	21.4	-33.7	-34.8
Turkmenia	271.88	32.2	16.9	5.8	17.3	-32.9
Estonia	-2.46	62.8	32.0	-16.9	-1.9	8.8
Without Clearing	441.0	2375.0	1008.0	1417.0	1033.0	1499.0
With Clearing	0.0	1462.0	80.0	982.0	919.0	1490.0

(*continued*)

TABLE 8.4 (*continued*)

Importing Republic	*Exporting Republic*			*Total Inter-republic*
	Armenia	*Turkmenia*	*Estonia*	*Imports*
Russia	423.1	198.5	-398.9	-
Ukraine	22.1	-246.7	-72.0	-
Belarus	-138.0	-51.7	-89.0	-
Uzbekistan	91.2	1238.3	-3.3	-
Kazakhstan	132.4	-41.2	44.0	-
Georgia	29.7	-75.1	3.5	-
Azerbaijan	-536.9	-271.9	2.5	-
Lithuania	-15.9	-32.2	-62.8	-
Moldova	-47.1	-16.9	-32.0	-
Latvia	-21.4	-5.8	16.9	-
Kyrgyzstan	33.7	-17.3	1.9	-
Tajikistan	34.8	32.9	-8.8	-
Armenia	0.0	-93.3	12.3	-
Turkmenia	93.3	0.0	-13.0	-
Estonia	-12.3	13.0	0.0	-
Without Clearing	772.0	852.0	680.0	32712
With Clearing	0.0	0.0	598.0	19643

TABLE 8.5 Bilateral Balances in Percent of Imports: Republics' Export and Import of Products for 1987

			Exporting Republic				
Importing Republic	*Russia*	*Ukraine*	*Belarus*	*Uzbekistan*	*Kazakhstan*	*Georgia*	
Azerbaijan							
Russia	8.48	0.00	2.87	-5.58	-4.93	-4.02	-2.59
Ukraine	0.26	-1.14	0.00	-2.69	-3.05	-0.89	-1.23
Belarus	1.57	1.70	2.06	0.00	3.88	3.71	2.60
Uzbekistan	7.57	1.85	2.88	-4.77	0.00	4.39	-3.74
Kazakhstan	-0.19	0.52	0.29	-1.56	-1.51	0.00	7.96
Georgia	-2.63	0.30	0.36	-1.00	1.17	-7.24	0.00
Azerbaijan	2.86	-0.07	1.84	-1.05	-0.68	0.49	-0.48
Lithuania	-0.72	2.01	0.87	0.20	-0.77	-1.01	-0.41
Moldova	0.85	-0.34	1.30	-0.73	-0.77	-0.05	-0.54
Latvia	1.02	0.10	0.16	-0.30	0.83	1.02	0.18
Kyrgyzstan	0.88	0.50	0.57	1.69	0.43	1.19	1.62
Tajikistan	-0.60	-0.05	0.83	-0.72	-0.85	-0.55	11.02
Armenia	-0.28	0.59	0.31	-9.75	0.26	1.40	5.58
Turkmenia	0.57	0.17	0.54	0.03	-0.28	-0.07	-0.05
Estonia	0.00	0.00	0.00	0.00	0.00	0.00	0.00
Total Inter-republic Exports	19.64	-8.13	13.79	-34.89	-40.30	0.81	57.78

(*continued*)

TABLE 8.5 (*continued*)

	Exporting Republic							
Importing Republic	*Lithuania*	*Moldova*	*Latvia*	*Kyrgyzstan*	*Tajikistan*	*Armenia*	*Turkmenia*	*Estonia*
Russia	0.37	-15.29	2.67	-1.26	-6.01	0.58	-9.01	-2.16
Ukraine	-4.17	-2.63	-4.05	-0.82	-2.72	-3.65	-1.89	-2.67
Belarus	1.83	-0.47	1.76	1.20	-6.16	2.41	45.26	-0.10
Uzbekistan	1.46	2.20	2.26	-4.06	-1.94	3.50	-1.50	1.32
Kazakhstan	-0.36	0.99	0.05	-1.71	-1.82	0.79	-2.74	0.10
Georgia	0.32	0.36	0.50	-0.27	-2.27	-14.20	-9.94	0.07
Azerbaijan	0.00	0.20	-9.51	0.74	-0.17	-0.42	-1.18	-1.88
Lithuania	-0.15	0.00	-1.50	-0.76	-0.58	-1.25	-0.62	-0.96
Moldova	6.93	1.45	0.00	0.11	-0.65	-0.57	-0.21	0.51
Latvia	-0.33	0.45	-0.06	0.00	-0.90	0.89	-0.63	0.06
Kyrgyzstan	0.08	0.37	0.43	0.98	0.00	0.92	1.20	-0.26
Tajikistan	0.22	0.86	0.40	-1.06	-1.00	0.00	-3.41	0.37
Armenia	0.44	0.31	0.11	0.54	-0.94	2.47	0.00	-0.39
Turkmenia	0.86	0.58	-0.32	-0.06	0.25	-0.33	0.48	0.00
Estonia	0.00	0.00	0.00	0.00	0.00	0.00	0.00	0.00
Total Inter-republic Exports	-20.09	-1.46	-18.51	-28.83	-42.72	2.35	23.05	-17.94

balances from Table 8.3 expressed as percentages of each republic's inter republic imports. Credits for each republic equal to 30 percent of their inter-republic imports would have allowed all but two of the small republics to remain well within their mechanism limits. Thirty percent is an arbitrary number, but it is roughly equal to the quotas in the European Currency Union and is equal to the import reserve ratio for developing countries.

The question remains, however, as to the likely dollar value of inter-republic trade during the first year of its operation. Table 8.6 shows the ruble value of quotas needed to provide each republic with coverage of 30 percent of imports assuming volumes and prices were equal to their 1987 levels. The equivalent dollar value would, of course, depend on the market exchange rate expected to prevail during the first year of the payments mechanism. The official dollar prices of rubles in 1987 was about $1.60. The second column in Table 8.6 shows the dollar value of quotas if this exchange rate prevailed.

It seems quite likely, however, that a real depreciation of the ruble will occur in the short run. In fact the apparent unwillingness of the West to provide large transfers to the Commonwealth states, along with their insistence on continued debt service, would suggest a sharp deterioration in the terms of trade as the Commonwealth states as a group make net exports to the rest of the world. Moreover, the volume of inter-republic trade will likely fall due to difficulties in coping with the reform process.

TABLE 8.6 Quotas for Mechanism (millions of rubles)

	Quotas (rubles) 30% of Imports	*Quota (US$) 1.6 × 1*	*Quota (US$) 0.5 × 1*	*Capital (US$) 0.1 × 2*
Russia	20161.71	32258.730	10080.850	3225.8730
Ukraine	10850.61	17360.970	5425.305	1736.0970
Belarus	4224.87	6759.792	2112.435	675.9792
Uzbekistan	3412.05	5459.280	1706.025	545.9280
Kazakhstan	4130.49	6608.784	2065.245	660.8784
Georgia	1442.97	2308.752	721.485	230.8752
Azerbaijan	1275.27	2040.432	637.635	204.0432
Lithuania	1757.85	2812.560	878.925	281.2560
Moldova	1429.71	2287.536	714.855	228.7536
Latvia	1387.83	2220.528	693.915	222.0528
Kyrgyzstan	834.27	1334.832	417.135	133.4832
Tajikistan	923.16	1477.056	461.580	147.7056
Armenia	984.54	1575.264	492.270	157.5264
Turkmenia	778.77	1246.032	389.385	124.6032
Estonia	891.96	1427.136	445.980	142.7136
Total Exports	54486.06	87177.690	27243.030	8717.7690

A possible source of information about the dollar value of the republics' trade can be obtained from valuations of their trade with Eastern European countries. Estimates are available for the value of trade between Hungary and the Commonwealth states as a group in 1990, valued both in rubles and forints. The ratio of these values suggests that the forint-ruble cross rate for this group of goods is about 27 forints per ruble. The market forint-dollar cross rate at the same time was about 62 forints per dollar. This suggests a "market" rate of $0.44 per ruble. A similar calculation for trade with Czechoslovakia suggests a rate of $0.50 per ruble. Column 4 of Table 8.6 shows the dollar value of quotas assuming a rate of $0.50 per ruble. We see no really useful way to refine these calculations. Perhaps it is unreasonable to regard the dollar amounts in Table 8.6 as providing a reasonable range for the credit lines required. Finally, we might guess that capital equal to 10 percent of quotas is needed to insure the credibility of the mechanism. Contributions from the West could take the form of guarantees for bonds issued by the mechanism.

References

Brabant, Jozef M. 1991. "Convertibility in Eastern Europe Through a Payments Union," in John Williamson, ed., *Currency Convertibility in Eastern Europe*. Pp. 63–95. Washington, D.C.: Institute for International Economics.

Dornbusch, Rudiger. 1991. "A Payments Mechanism for the Soviet Union and Eastern Europe." Mimeo. Cambridge: MIT, November.

Gros, Daniel. 1991. "A Soviet Payments Union?" Mimeo. Brussels: Center for European Policy Studies, November.

Havrylyshen, Oley, and John Williamson. 1991. *From Soviet Disunion to Eastern Economic Community?* Washington, D.C.: Institute for International Economics.

Kenen, Peter. 1991. "Transitional Arrangements for Trade and Payments Among the CMEA Countries." *IMF Staff Papers* 38(2): 236–67.

Williamson, John. 1992. *Trade and Payments After Soviet Disintegration*. Washington, D.C.: Institute for International Economics.

About the Editors and Contributors

Kalman Dezseri is a Research Fellow at the Institute for World Economics in Budapest.

David G. Dickinson is Senior Lecturer in Economics and Director of the Money, Banking and Finance Programs at the University of Birmingham, England.

Michael Dooley is Professor of Economics at the University of California, Santa Cruz and Research Associate at the National Bureau for Economic Research.

Manuel Guitián is Director of the Monetary and Exchange Affairs Department, International Monetary Fund.

Andy W. Mullineux is Professor of Money and Banking in the Department of Economics and Head of the School of Social Sciences at the University of Birmingham, England.

Christine P. Ries is Professor of Economics and Chair of the School of Economics, Ivan Allen College, Georgia Institute of Technology.

Richard J. Sweeney is Sullivan/Dean Professor of International Finance at the Georgetown School of Business, Georgetown University.

Clas Wihlborg is Felix Neubergh Professor of Banking and Financial Economics at the School of Economics and Commercial Law, Göteborg University.

John Williamson is Chief Economist for the South Asia Region at the World Bank, Washington, D.C.

Thomas D. Willett is Horton Professor of Economics, Claremont McKenna College and The Claremont Graduate School.